The Technique of
TENERIFFE LACE

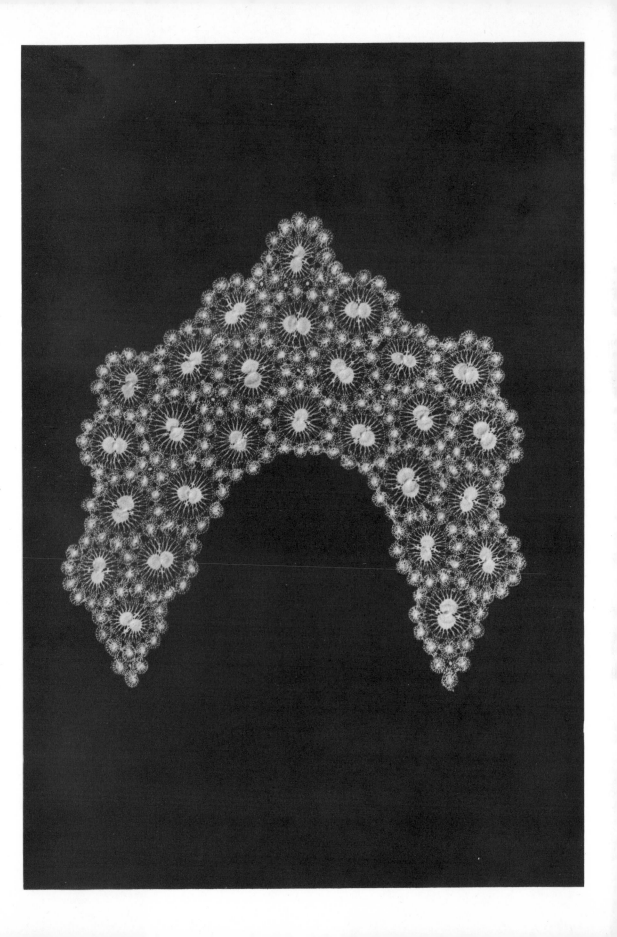

The Technique of
TENERIFFE LACE

Alexandra Stillwell

B T Batsford Ltd   London

© Alexandra Stillwell 1980
First published 1980
ISBN 0 7134 2193 2
All rights reserved. No part of
this publication may be
reproduced, in any form or by
any means, without permission
from the publishers
Set in Monophoto Plantin
10 on 12 pt by
Willmer Brothers Ltd, Birkenhead
Printed by The Anchor Press Ltd
Tiptree, Essex
for the publishers
B T Batsford Limited
4 Fitzhardinge Street, London
W1H 0AH

Contents

Introduction

During the last few years there has been a great revival in the finer, more delicate forms of needlework and lacemaking. Many people, of all ages, now have the interest and determination not only to try intricate work but to learn it properly and be satisfied only with work of the highest standard.

Much of my knowledge of fine needlework and lacemaking was culled from books during the late 1950s and the 1960s when such work was out of fashion. It was during my delving into old books and magazines that I first met Teneriffe lace and I could not resist trying it. This branch of craft work was more difficult than most to track down; very little has been written on the subject, mainly magazine articles and the occasional chapter in old needlework books. The rest has been gained from the examination of pieces of lace and gleaned from elderly ladies who remember making it as children. However, there have been few who have made it since the war.

Like many other crafts this one has been through the doldrums. The wheels, curved needles and netting shuttles that were formerly used have not been obtainable for many years; and most of those that have survived are in collections. My first attempts were made on wheels consisting of corrugated cardboard and pins; becoming frustrated with the disadvantages of this type I modified it until it evolved into the one described in chapter 2. It is easy to make from readily available materials and is convenient and versatile in use.

Chapter 3 is devoted to a detailed description of the making of a single medallion and the joining of seven similar pieces into a mat. This design contains the three basic stitches of Teneriffe lace and the following chapter gives the variations on these stitches, with examples showing them in use. Try copying them at first—then experiment. Techniques typical of Sol lace have also been included; the making of the lace is similar although the development has occurred separately.

Lace is a fabric containing both open and close work giving the appearance of light and shade; it is the balance and harmony of these that determine the success of the design. Chapter 5 is concerned with the making of plans, chapter 6 explores different shapes and their corresponding webs, and to assist in their preparation there are some polar co-ordinate papers in the appendix.

Chapters 7 and 8 are concerned with modern developments and the use of medallions. They can be made on a large scale, using textured threads and mixtures of colours but care should be taken to ensure that the overall appearance does not become too cluttered. Details of many other wheels are to be found in chapter 9. Some are more convenient to use than others! When pins are being used vertically, 2.5 cm (1 in) pins can be used, then, after the first medallion has been worked, it can be covered with a piece of paper the size of the medallion and another worked on top. In this way up to six can be worked before removing the pins—quite a time saver.

I wish to express my thanks to all my friends and students who have encouraged me to write this book, especially Angela Parker who first talked me into it, Sheila Daeth who tried out my instructions, Alan Meck A.I.I.P. who did the photography and, above all, Grace Bevan for her constant help and encouragement. My thanks also go to Carter and Parker Ltd, for their help concerning the Wendy multi-needle and Twilleys of Stamford for their co-operation concerning the flower loom.

CHAPTER 1

Teneriffe Lace, its Ancestors and Relatives

The origins of modern Teneriffe lace are to be found in the embroidery of the Middle Ages. Very little lace, as we know it, was made at that time; the majority of early work resulting in a 'lacy' appearance was cut work or drawn thread work and it is from these that the modern Teneriffe lace evolved.

When a band of threads is withdrawn from a woven fabric it leaves a 'ladder' of loose threads which, in drawn thread work, are embroidered and grouped together to form a decorative band. When drawn thread embroidery is worked round an article such as a tray cloth, threads are withdrawn in bands all round. When one of these bands joins or crosses another, an empty square is produced. This square can be filled by laying a web of threads across it and embroidering over them to form a spider's web (figures 1, 2 and 3).

Over the years these spider's web fillings became more and more elaborate, the bands of work became wider and the corners larger. The embroidery in the corners became more stylised and developed into a medallion. This form of embroidery was very popular throughout Europe, especially in Spain, during the sixteenth century. By then the corners had become an important feature of the work, not merely a method of filling in the inevitable square occurring in drawn thread work (figures 4 and 5).

The technique of embroidering a web of threads became adapted for cutwork. A circle, square or other shape was drawn on linen mounted in an embroidery frame. A web was then laid across points marked around the circle and the embroidery worked. A line of buttonhole stitching was worked along the edge of the design to finish off the linen and to support the web threads, after which the linen behind the medallion was carefully cut away (figures 6 and 7).

This type of embroidery was especially popular in Spain during the sixteenth and seventeenth centuries where the medallions are known as 'sol' (sun) or 'rueda' (wheel) designs. Of course the stitches used to decorate the cutwork medallions are those to be found in drawn thread work.

In Spain, probably during the sixteenth century, the background fabric of the cutwork was dispensed with. A web was stretched across a circle, square or other shaped outline of running stitches worked in a piece of linen which may or may not have been mounted in an embroidery frame. (It is definitely easier to do this type of work in a frame, but not essential if the running stitches are worked through several thicknesses of stiff linen.) Embroidery stitches, still those characteristic of drawn thread work, were used to decorate the web. When the medallion was complete the running stitches in the linen were cut and the medallion set free. The cutwork 'sol' embroidery had developed into a lace—which is by definition 'fine open fabric of linen, cotton, silk, woollen or metal threads usually with inwrought or applied patterns' (Concise Oxford Dictionary). This style became popular in Spain and is known as Spanish 'Sol' lace (figures 8 and 9).

At some time during the sixteenth century the technique of making this lace was carried to South America. Some authorities favour the theory that the Conquistadors were the carriers; others the Jesuits. At this time in history lace and other decorative types of handwork were made by both men and women. It is highly probable that some of the Conquistadors were skilled in this craft and used it to while away the time on board the sailing ships that took them across the Atlantic. Conditions on these sailing ships were very cramped and little room could be spared for pastimes. As this form of lacemaking can be made on a linen ground without a frame it would need little room and not much equipment. The equipment required would be a piece of linen to work on (the same one could be used for many pieces of lace), a spool of thread and a needle. These men could have passed on the skills of the craft to the local inhabitants after they had landed. On the other hand, female camp followers or Spanish ladies may have disseminated the craft when they accompanied the men on later expeditions.

The Jesuits also travelled from Spain to South America in the sixteenth century. They demanded a high standard of ornamentation on the Church linens, and one way of obtaining this was to teach the local population the necessary skills required. Thus by one or more of these routes the technique of making Sol lace arrived in South America.

It was in South America that the style of Sol lace developed further, becoming more delicate, the designs relying more on the interplay of light and shade of loose threads and close weaving than on the intricacy of the stitches. In fact, the vast majority of the work was now done in knot stitch and darning only.

The laces of Bolivia, Brazil and Peru retained the name of Sol lace, but in Paraguay it became known as 'ñanduti' from a Guaranian word meaning 'web'. Here the filmy lace started its life as a design marked in pencil on a piece of linen stretched across a wooden frame. Outlines of running stitches were worked round the circles and other shaped parts of the design and webs stretched across them as in the Spanish Sol lace. These were then embroidered. Odd shaped spaces were worked with a web of threads running at right angles to each other rather than radially. These, typical of ñanduti work, were also embroidered. The completed piece of work, or section, was set free by removing the running stitches.

Diagram 1 indicates the positions of the seams joining the twelve large sections that make up the border of the Paraguayan tablecloth (figures 16, 17 and 18). The sections have been oversewn together.

The two collars in figures 21 and 22 were made, to order, by the same person but are each quite different in style. Figure 21 shows work typical of an enthusiastic craft worker who enjoys the craft. There is the maximum amount of variety at the expense of true symmetry. The second collar in figure 22 has been made with a definite effort to achieve symmetry—more thought for the final appearance at the expense of the enjoyment. Both collars have the same sized medallions and spaces between them, so it is fairly safe to assume that both were made on the same pattern, a great time saver for the worker. Both are rich in the designs of the medallions and fillings and the work is of a very high standard.

Tradition has it that a seventeenth-century lacemaker in Tenerife replaced the foundation of running stitches with a circle of pins set in a firm pincushion. The web was stretched across these pins and the embroidery worked over this web. The completed medallion was released by removing the pins. This is the method still used today by lacemakers in Tenerife where the craft continues as a cottage industry (figure 23). (It will be noted that, although the modern spelling for the name of the island is Tenerife, the traditional spelling for the lace is Teneriffe, and it is this spelling which is used throughout this book.)

With changes in fashion and the invention of lacemaking machines, at the end of the eighteenth century, the handmade lace industry in Europe steadily declined. Lacemakers, whatever their technique, generally responded by using coarser thread in an attempt to compete with the lower prices of the machine-made article. This may have been an important factor in the development of the bold designs worked in relatively coarse thread that are now popular. Today's designs rely more on the grouping of the threads and less on the embroidery (figure 24).

Colour now plays an important part. Most laces are made from white thread and rely on the interplay of light and shade in the work to produce the decorative effect. Colour is, however, frequently used in modern Teneriffe work.

Figure 1
Preparation for drawn thread

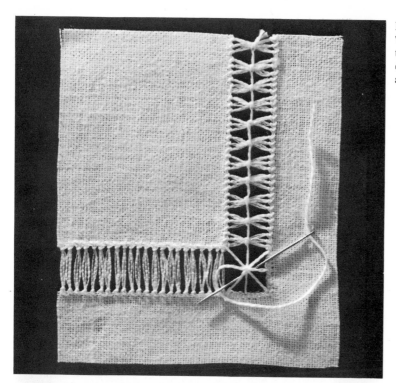

Figure 2
Working an insertion in drawn
thread work: the threads are
carried across the corner to form
a spider

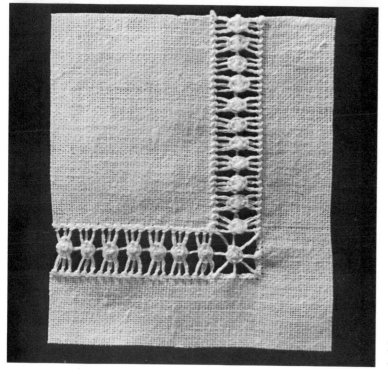

Figure 3
A spider's web insertion

Figure 4
A pillowcase decorated with
drawn thread work (from the
collection of the Embroiderers'
Guild)

Figure 5
Detail of the pillowcase: an
elaborate medallion motif and a
smaller square motif

Figure 6
Prepared linen with a web being
stretched for a cutwork medallion

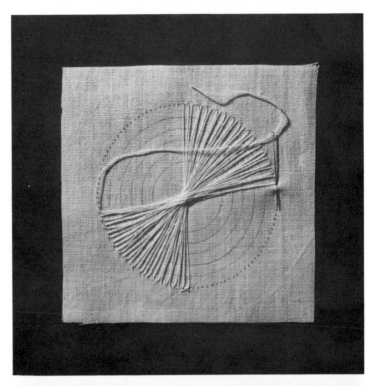

Figure 7
A completed cutwork medallion

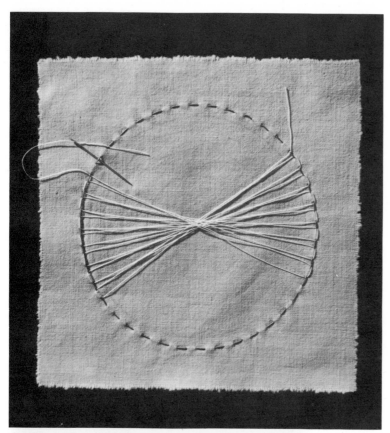

Figure 8
Stretching the web for Sol lace

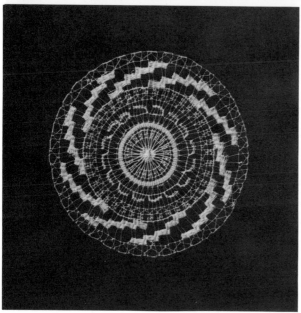

Figure 9
Sol lace

Figure 10
A handkerchief trimmed with
Paraguayan ñanduti (from the
collection of the Embroiderers'
Guild)

Figure 11
The butterfly corner of the
Paraguayan handkerchief
in figure 10

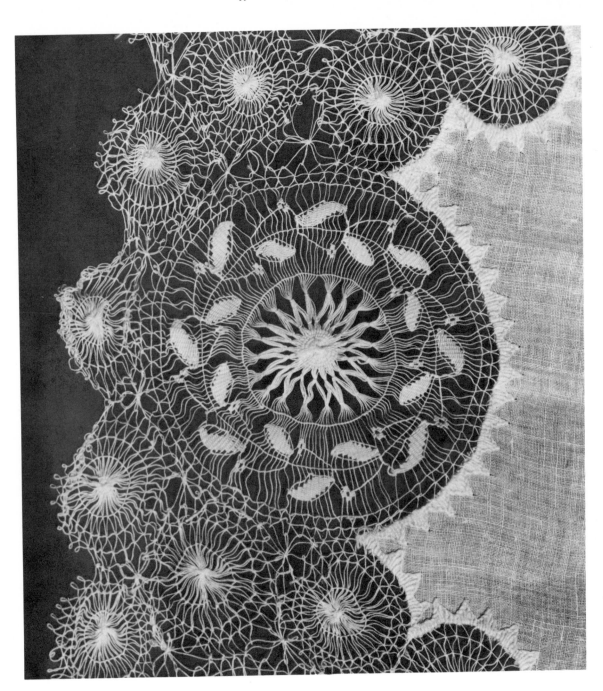

Figure 12
A motif of the Paraguayan
handkerchief in figure 10

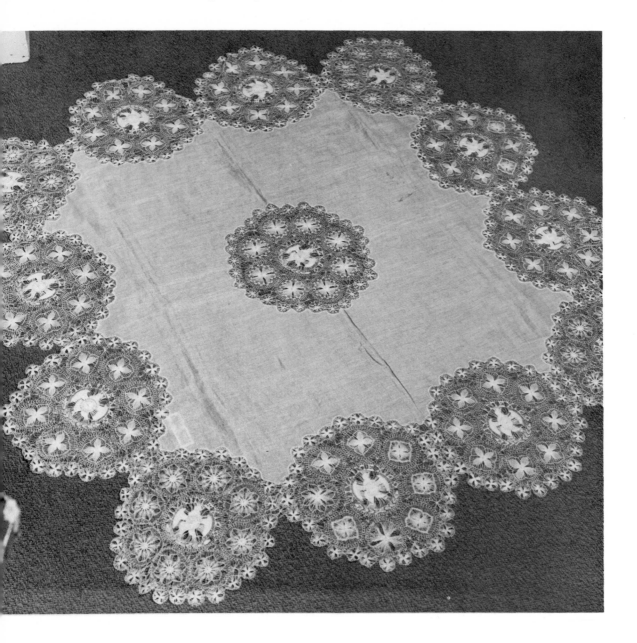

Figure 13
A Mexican tablecloth with Sol
lace trimming (from the collection
of the Embroiderers' Guild)

Figure 14
A large medallion of the Mexican
tablecloth in figure 13: the
Mexican eagle is surrounded by
the words 'Viva Mexico'

Figure 15
The central motif of the Mexican
tablecloth in figure 13: again the
Mexican eagle is surrounded by
the words 'Viva Mexico'

Figure 16
A tablecloth trimmed with
Paraguayan ñanduti (from the
collection of the Embroiderers'
Guild)

Diagram 1
Plan of the Paraguayan tablecloth
in figure 16: the dotted lines
indicate the seams joining the
large sections

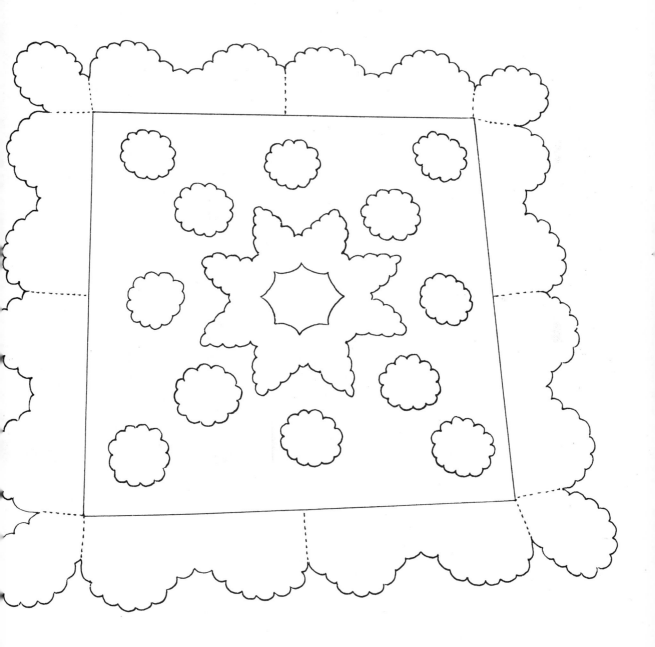

Figure 17
The corner of the tablecloth in
figure 16

Figure 18
A detail of the Paraguayan
tablecloth in figure 16

Figure 19
The centre of the tablecloth in
figure 16

Figure 20
A circular motif of the
Paraguayan tablecloth in figure 16

Figure 21
A collar in Paraguayan ñanduti

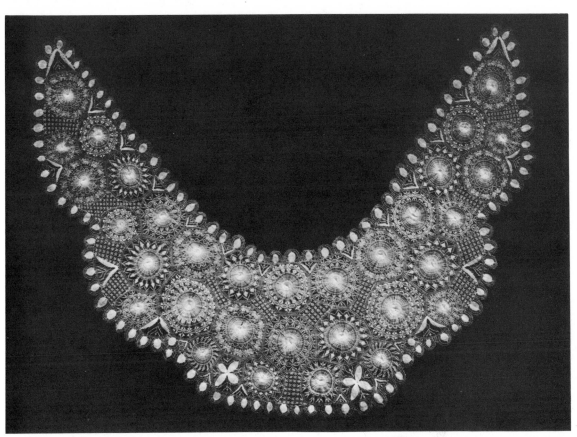

Figure 22
A collar in Paraguayan ñanduti

Figure 23
Using a pincushion to support the
web

Figure 24
Modern lace from Tenerife

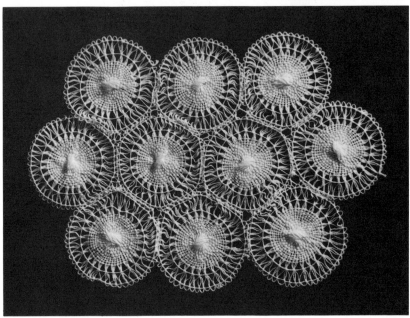

Figure 25
Lace made in Tenerife
during the early twentieth century
(from the collection of Mrs Joan
Tyler)

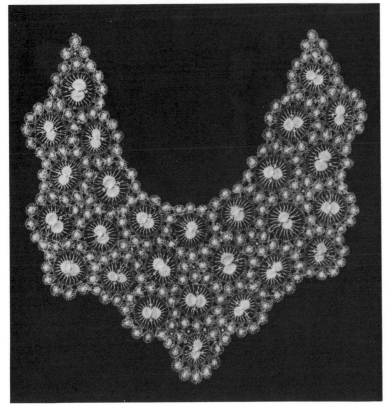

Figure 26
A lace collar from Tenerife made
during the early twentieth century
(from the collection of Mrs Joan
Tyler)

CHAPTER 2
Basic Tools and Materials

Figure 27
Equipment and materials for making Teneriffe lace; the netting shuttle and curved needles are no longer manufactured

THE TENERIFFE WHEEL

Teneriffe lace is always made on a lace wheel or other foundation across which a web of threads is laid and supported while the decorative embroidery is worked. A descriptive list of many varieties of lace wheel is given in chapter 9, together with illustrations and instructions for making them where applicable. To begin with, however, instructions are given here for making a simple, versatile and inexpensive wheel using foam plastic and pins.

Foam plastic pad

A simple wheel can be made from spongy, polyurethane foam plastic, 2 cm ($\frac{3}{4}$ in) thick, preferably a piece with the skin that forms during its manufacture still present on one side. The skin makes the foundation more firm to work on. For the simple lace medallion described in the next chapter, a pad 7.5 × 7.5 cm (3 × 3 in) is required. The square can be drawn on the skin of the plastic foam using a ball-point pen, and can be cut out with a sharp craft knife or razor blade mounted in a handle. This process is rendered easier if a steel rule or other straight edge is laid along the line and pressed down hard to squash the foam as flat as possible. The foam can then be cut right through the first time (figure 29).

This technique of using foam plastic for the wheel or the foundation can be utilised for almost any shape and design of medallion, and the pad made can be re-used for as long as it remains in good condition. For most medallions the foam plastic pad should

Figure 28
A Teneriffe wheel

be 0.5 cm ($\frac{1}{4}$ in) larger all round than the design with a minimum size of 7.5 × 7.5 cm (3 × 3 in). A smaller foam plastic pad is not as easy to hold.

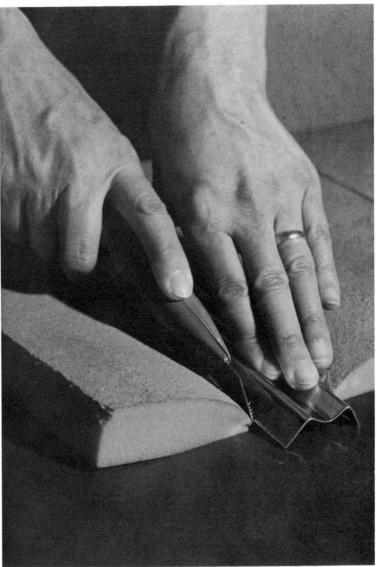

Figure 29
Cutting polyurethane foam with a craft knife and a safety rule

Pins

Pins used for lace work, no matter what type, should always be non-rusting so as to avoid staining the threads. They are usually made of brass, yellow or white, or stainless steel. For use with the foam plastic pad described in this chapter, the 1.3 cm ($\frac{1}{2}$ in) brass lace and silk pins known as "Lills" are excellent. They are non-rusting and short enough not to protrude through the pad.

Plan

With the type of wheel being described here a wheel plan can be used. This is a paper pattern which shows the positions of the pins (i.e. the dots) and has concentric circles marked to provide guidelines when working the embroidery.

The plan shown here (diagram 2) is for the simple medallion described in the following chapter. Both the dots and the guidelines should be transferred onto notepaper (bond or cartridge paper) of medium thickness. To do this, use tracing paper to trace the plan from the page, then use a light carbon paper (i.e. a type which will not leave unwanted smudges on the paper underneath) to transfer the lines onto the clean sheet of thick paper. Some notepaper is made fine enough for the guidelines to be seen through it; this allows the design to be traced straight from the page without the need for carbon paper. The plan should then be trimmed with scissors so that it is just a little smaller than the foam plastic pad.

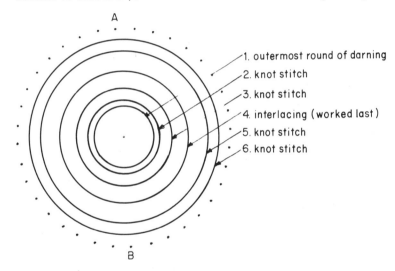

1. outermost round of darning
2. knot stitch
3. knot stitch
4. interlacing (worked last)
5. knot stitch
6. knot stitch

Diagram 2
The plan of the medallion in figure 31, described in chapter 3

Assembling the wheel

The plan is placed on the foam pad and held in place by a pin pushed through the spot in the centre. A pin is now pushed into the foam pad through every dot of the outer circle on the plan. When a pin has been placed in every dot, the pin in the centre should be removed. The heads of the pins should be left slightly raised, by about 3 mm ($\frac{1}{8}$ in), until after the web has been stretched. They are then pushed flush with the surface.

THREAD

The thread should be smooth. Most lace, embroidery and crochet threads can be used for this type of work, but care should be taken to choose one of a suitable thickness bearing in mind the size of the design and the number of pins. The threads most widely used are perle embroidery thread Nos 5–12, with No. 8 being the most popular, and crochet cotton Nos 3–150 with No. 20 being the most popular.

As with all laces, white, ecru and occasionally black are the traditional colours with each piece worked in a single colour. Two-colour work is now becoming popular with white and ecru being the favourites for forming the web and some or all of the embroidery being worked in a contrasting colour. However, care must be taken when introducing a second colour as it adds a new dimension to the work, and as in other types of lace, the colour tends to become the dominant factor, overwhelming the intricacy of the work. White with ecru and pink on white can give very pleasing results, while black on white can be both startling and effective. Try experimenting with different combinations.

NEEDLES

Formerly fine netting shuttles or long curved needles were used, but if these are not obtainable a straight needle must be used. It should be blunt, as a sharp point would 'spear' the threads and spoil the effect. The needle should be as long as possible.

CHAPTER 3
A Simple Lace Medallion

The lace mat in figure 30 is composed of seven lace medallions linked with an oversewing stitch. Chapter 2 gives instructions for making a suitable wheel and plan (diagram 2). Also needed for these medallions are a blunt needle and No. 8 perle embroidery thread.

Figure 30
A mat made from simple medallions

39

Figure 31
A simple Teneriffe medallion
used to make the mat in figure 30

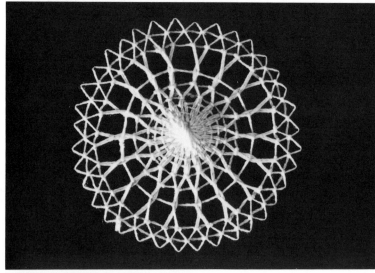

Figure 31
A simple Teneriffe medallion
used to make the mat in figure 30

STRETCHING THE WEB

Unwind a length of thread from the ball (do not cut any off) and, using a needle, pass it through the central point of the plan and foam plastic pad from front to back. After removing the needle make a knot in the thread to prevent it from pulling out. Gently pull the thread so that the knot just touches the pad. Take the thread, coming from the ball, in the right hand (do not cut any off yet) and pass it round pin A (diagram 3). Now take it across the wheel and round the opposite pin B (diagram 3). Take the thread across the plan and round the pin next to pin A (diagram 4), then back and round the opposite pin (diagram 5).

Diagram 3
Stretching the web around the
first two pins

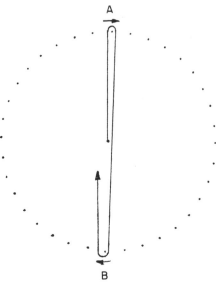

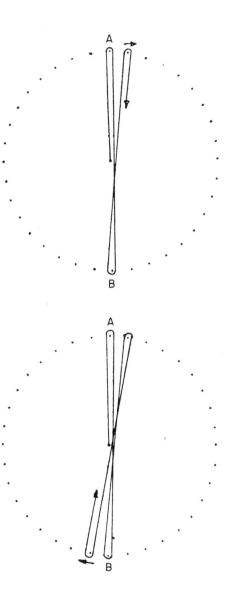

Diagram 4
Stretching the web around the third pin

Diagram 5
Stretching the web around the fourth pin

Continue winding thread round until all the pins have been used. After passing the thread round the last pin, secure it by taking it across the pad and twice round a pin pushed into the side of the pad. Provided this pin is pushed deep into the foam it will hold.

Now cut the thread 120 cm (48 in) from the foam pad and thread the end through a tapestry needle. Although this long thread may cause some difficulty (namely getting caught on everything in sight!) until some has been used, it will enable you to complete the embroidery without having to join in extra threads. Now push all the pins into the foam pad so that they will not catch the thread.

DARNING THE CENTRE

Hold the last thread crossing the centre of the web onto the centre with your left thumb to stop it unwinding. Release the thread held temporarily by the pin in the side of the pad and work the first round of darning.

Pass the needle under the pair of threads supported by pin B, over the next pair on the left, under the next pair and over the next, keeping the web threads in their pairs all the time, until the round is complete.

When the second round of darning is worked the needle must go over the threads it went under during the first round, and under the threads it previously went over. The change can be made when pair B is reached at the end of the first round. The needle can pick up the first thread only of the pair and pass over the other thread.

It is now ready to pass under and over the following pairs. This pattern requires a total of four rounds of double darning with the last round just reaching the inner circle (ring 1) on the plan. Finish the darning by passing the needle under the darning thread of the previous round just before pair B (diagram 6).

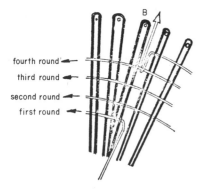

fourth round
third round
second round
first round

Diagram 6
Anchoring the thread at the end
of the darning

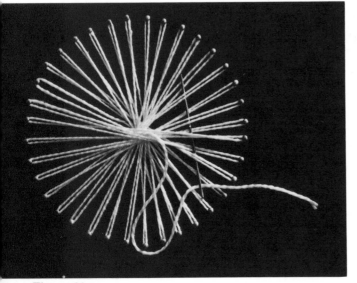

Figure 32
Starting the darned centre

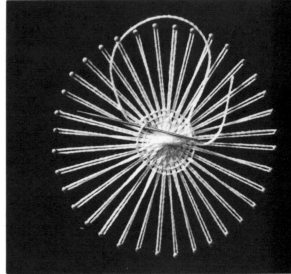

Figure 33
Anchoring the thread after
darning

KNOT STITCH

Work one round of knot stitch on ring 2 of the plan, grouping two pairs of threads together each time. Start with pair B and the next pair on the left.

Work one knot round them. (Diagram 7 shows how the knot is worked.) Work another knot round the next two pairs on the left, and so on all round. Finish the knots by working a knot over the first one of the round. Pass the thread to the next round, ring 3, on the plan, by laying it along the web threads of the pair on the left of B, knot

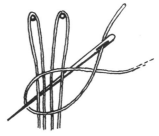

Diagram 7
Working a knot

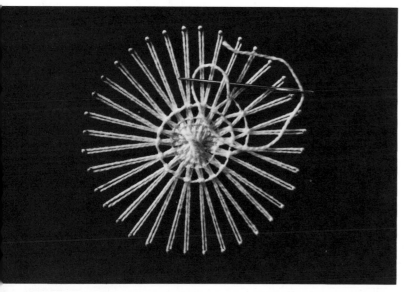

Figure 34
Starting the second round of knot stitch

this pair and the pair to the left together. Continue until the round has been completed and finish off as for the previous round.

Ring 4 on the plan shows the position of the round of interlacing, but this is to be worked last, after the rounds worked on rings 5 and 6 of the plan. The round worked on ring 5 knots the threads in their original pairs, and on ring 6 the knots regroup the threads, taking one thread from each of the two adjacent pairs.

Finish by knotting on top of the first knot of the round. The remainder of the thread is now cut off. A tiny dab of fabric adhesive applied with a pin will prevent the knot from working loose, but take care to choose an adhesive which will not be affected when the lace is washed and laundered.

INTERLACING

The last round of embroidery is the interlacing worked on ring 4. Take a length of thread in the needle and pass the needle from left to right behind the left-hand pair of the two pairs grouped on ring 3. Now pass the needle over the pair on the right of it, i.e. the other pair of the group (diagram 8).

Rest the point of the needle on the pad and move the eye end to the right (diagram 9). The point now slides under both pairs towards the left and the needle is laid down (diagram 10). Finish the stitch by pushing the needle through between the threads and pulling until the interlacing thread is just becoming taut, keeping the pairs crossed. Repeat this stitch with the group of two pairs on the left and so on until the round has been completed. Tie the ends together with a reef knot and cut off the threads.

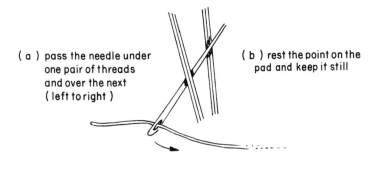

(a) pass the needle under one pair of threads and over the next (left to right)

(b) rest the point on the pad and keep it still

(c) lift this end and move it in the direction of the arrow

Diagram 8
Starting the interlacing

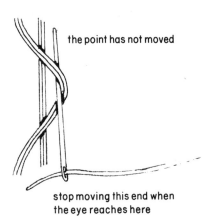

the point has not moved

stop moving this end when the eye reaches here

Diagram 9
Crossing the threads in interlacing

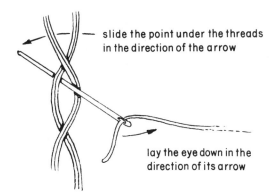

slide the point under the threads
in the direction of the arrow

lay the eye down in the
direction of its arrow

Diagram 10
The threads crossed in interlacing

RELEASING

Before the medallion can be set free you must cut off the knot at the back
of the pad; then remove the pins from around the edge and pull the
central thread out of the pad, taking care that it does not pull the
work. This thread can be cut off close to the work as it does not
require fastening off. The 'right side' of the medallion is the one
that faced the plan while it was being made. Although this is a
general rule the other side may be more effective in appearance, and
if so, should be used as the 'right side'.

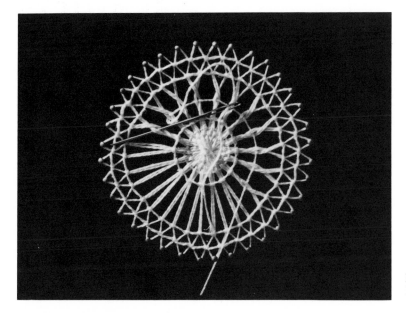

Figure 35
Interlacing

MAKING A SMALL MAT

Now you have completed your first medallion you only need
another six (you should get faster each time) to make the small mat

in figure 30. To join the medallions, hold two pieces, numbers 1 and 2 (diagram 11), with right sides together and their looped edges in line. Fasten on by passing a needle, threaded with the same thread as the web, through one pair of loops and tie a single knot to fasten the two loops together. Do not cut off the end.

Continue by oversewing one stitch through each of the next two pairs of loops. The two medallions are joined by three loops each. This is marked A–B on diagram 11. Now work B–C by oversewing along the last line of knot stitch of medallion 2, working one stitch round each of the straight threads forming the inner side of the next three loops.

Now hold medallion 3 against medallion 2, with right sides facing. Oversew the next three pairs of loops, C–D. Oversew back to C without repeating the stitch in the last pair at D but only the other two. Work the next three loops, C–E (as for B–C).

Now join medallions 1 and 3 from E–F as follows: place these two medallions with right sides together and oversew the next loop of medallion 3 to the fourth loop from B of medallion 1. Continue working in the directions of the arrows. Finish by oversewing along the three loops to A. Tie the ends in a reef knot and cut them off.

Diagram 11
Joining the medallions

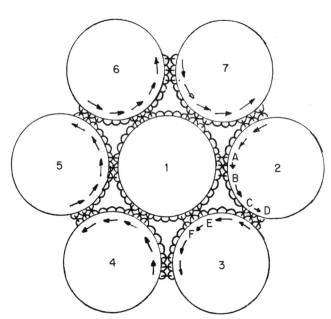

CHAPTER 4

Stitches and Edgings

Darning in one form or another is one of the basic stitches of this type of work and usually forms the first rows worked around the centre of a medallion. The darning round the centre usually commences by passing the needle under the thread or threads that were first laid down.

DARNED CENTRES

Single darning

See diagram 12 and figure 36. The needle passes over one thread, under the next, over the next and so on until the round is complete. The second row is usually started by passing the needle under or over two threads so that it will then continue by passing over the threads it went under in the previous round and vice versa.

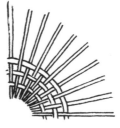

Figure 36
A centre in single darning

Diagram 12
Single darning

47

Double darning

See diagram 13 and figure 37. This is worked as for single darning but the needle passes over and under double threads, usually the pair of threads supported by one pin, but not necessarily so. Change rounds by splitting a pair and passing the needle over and under single threads just once.

Figure 37
A centre in double darning

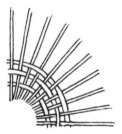

Diagram 13
Double darning

Group darning

See diagram 14 and figure 38. The web threads are divided into an odd number of groups and the needle darned under and over the groups. This method results in the web showing division into groups.

Figure 38
A centre in grouped darning and a darned band worked round the medallion

Diagram 14
Group darning

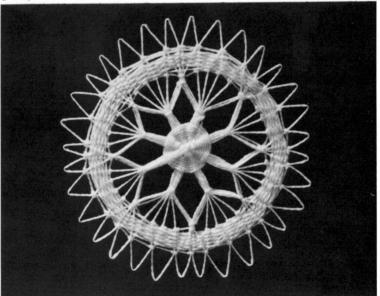

Back stitched centre

See diagram 15 and figure 39. The threads are divided into groups and the needle taken under, back over and under each group in turn.

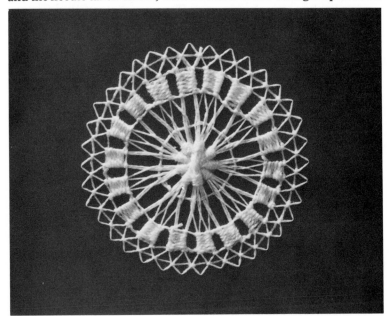

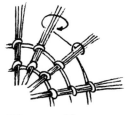

Figure 39
A back stitched centre

Diagram 15
Back stitch for the centre

Progressive darning

See diagram 16 and figure 40. The threads are divided into an even number of groups containing three or more threads. Each row the groups are advanced by one or more threads to form a spiral.

Figure 40
A centre in progressive darning

Diagram 16
Progressive darning

Darned bands

Darning is also used to decorate the web. Two rounds of knot stitch are worked and a band of darning worked between them; this band of darning may be worked round the web, as in diagram 17 and figure 38, or radially between the two rounds of knot stitches, as in diagram 18 and figure 47.

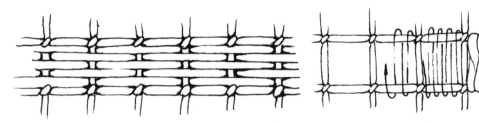

Diagram 17
A darned band worked around the web

Diagram 18
A darned band worked radially

DARNED SHAPES

Darning can also be used to form solid shapes within the medallion. These can take many forms. The simplest is the darned block which can be very effective when worked step fashion.

Darned blocks

In the sketch, four rounds of knot stitch have been worked with the knots around the same pairs of threads to form a series of square spaces across which the blocks can be worked (diagram 19, figure 41). These blocks can be worked without the rounds of knot stitches between the blocks (diagram 20, figure 42). In both cases there should be the same number of rows per block. Blocks can be worked radially (diagram 21), but these are not as common (figure 43).

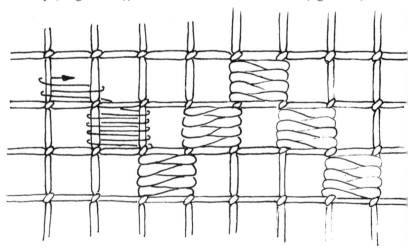

Diagram 19
Darned blocks

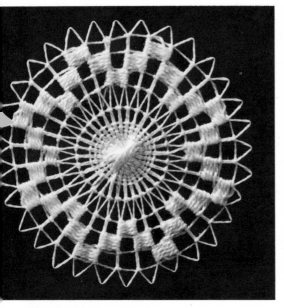

Figure 41
Stepped blocks with knot stitch
rounds between the blocks

Figure 42
Stepped blocks without the
intervening rounds of knot stitch

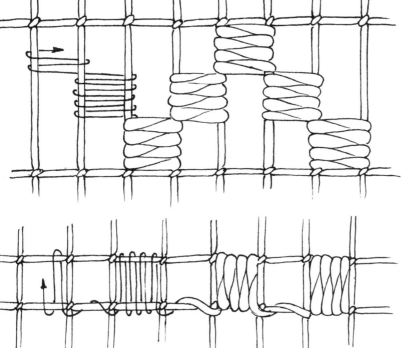

Diagram 20
Darned blocks without the
intervening rounds of knot stitch

Diagram 21
Darned blocks worked radially

Figure 43
Radially darned blocks and a
combination edge

Darning across triangular spaces

The outer round of knot stitch groups the threads in pairs, the inner
round splits alternate pairs and knots are worked to unite a single
thread to each side of the intervening pair; this creates a triangular
space. The darning is worked across this space from base to apex
(diagram 22, figure 44).

Alternatively one round of knot stitch can be worked with each
knot around a single thread. Work the darning around the required
number of threads, pulling the darning thread after each row to
reduce the width as the darning progresses (diagram 23). The
triangle finishes with a knot at the apex around the web threads used
for the triangle (figure 45).

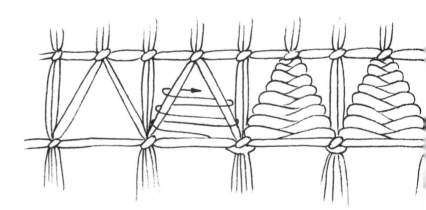

Diagram 22
Darning across triangular spaces

Figure 44
Darning across triangular spaces

Diagram 23
Darned triangles

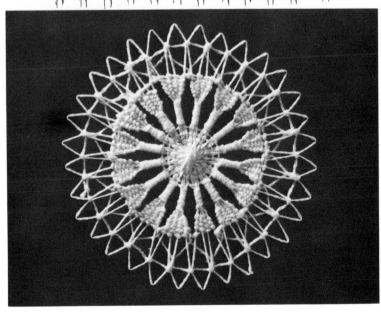

Figure 45
Darned triangles

Darned triangles on a gradually reduced number of threads

The triangle is worked from base to apex starting with several rows of single darning passing back and forth. Then one or more web threads are left out and one or more rows worked across the remainder. More threads are left out and more darning is worked. This is repeated until no more threads are left. The working thread is then taken down across the work to the base of the next triangle. This side of the work must be the back so that the thread passing from the apex of one triangle to the base of the next does not show on the front of the finished article (diagram 24, figure 46).

This method of throwing out threads to reduce the width of the darning and also taking in threads to increase the width can be used in different ways to create many forms including petal shapes and even butterflies. This technique is widely used in the South American Sol laces.

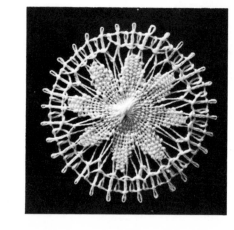

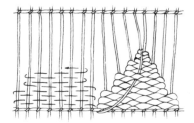

Diagram 24
Darned triangles

Figure 46
Darned triangles and a
picot edge

Darned semicircles

See diagram 25 and figure 47. For this the web threads must be pre-grouped by two rounds of knot stitch. One round groups the threads in pairs, the other regroups the threads in pairs with one thread from each of two adjacent pairs of the previous row. The semicircle is then darned across one of the knots, working first one way and then the other across the threads meeting at that knot.

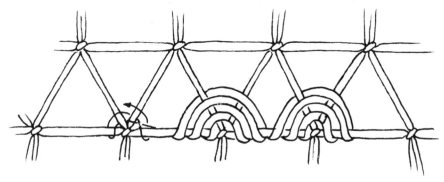

Diagram 25
Darned semicircles

Figure 47
Darned semicircles and a darned
band worked radially

Large darned rosettes

These are darned along a line of knot stitch that has pregrouped the
threads as for darned semicircles with five threads or pairs meeting
at each knot. The darning is worked around this junction. When the
required number of rounds of darning have been worked the needle
can be taken under the working thread of the knot stitch round
before working the next rosette (diagram 26, figure 48).

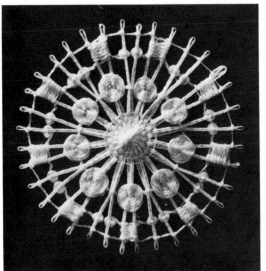

Figure 48
Darned rosettes

Diagram 26
Large darned rosettes

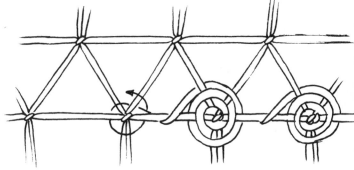

Small darned rosettes

These are worked around the knots of a round of knot stitch that has only four threads or pairs meeting at each knot. The working thread of the rosette passes over and under the same threads in each round. The thread is taken to the next rosette as for the large rosette (diagram 27, figure 48).

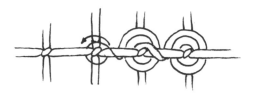

Diagram 27
Small darned rosettes

Diagram 28
Darned bars

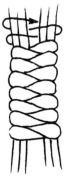

Darned bars

See diagram 28 and figure 49. The web threads to be used for the bar are divided in two groups and darned until the desired length has been reached. If required the needle can be taken down through the bar before passing on to the next one.

Bound bars

Another bar can be made by taking the thread round and round the same group of threads binding them together (diagram 29, figure 49).

Diagram 29
Bound bars

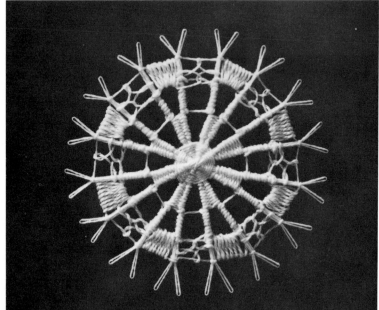

Figure 49
Darned and bound bars

INTERLACING

The simplest form requires the threads to be pregrouped into corresponding groups by two rounds of knot stitch. The interlacing then splits the groups, causing each thread to cross one from the adjacent group (diagram 30, figure 50).

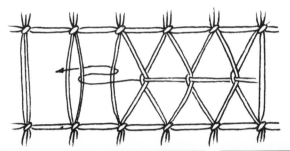

Diagram 30
Interlacing

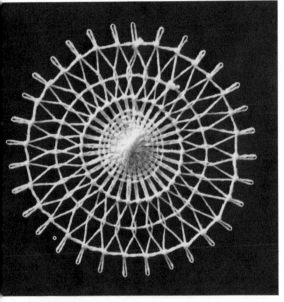

Figure 50
Interlacing

Figure 51
Interlacing in groups

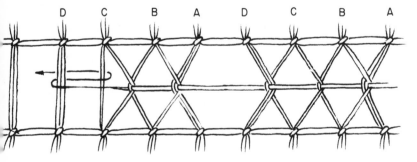

Diagram 31
Interlacing in groups

Interlacing in groups

See diagram 31 and figure 51. The threads need to be pregrouped by two rounds of knot stitch as described above. The threads are sometimes taken as separate threads and sometimes in pairs as grouped by the knots. Diagram 31 shows the pair A crossed over a single thread from B. The other thread from B crosses a single thread from C. The other thread from C crosses both threads D. There is a gap between D and the next pair A without any interlacing. Repeat from A to continue the round. The diagram shows four sets of two threads forming the interlaced groups but three or more than four sets may be used.

Double rounds of interlacing

The web needs to be pregrouped by two rounds of knot stitch, with the pairs regrouped in the second round, i.e. each pair of the second round is composed of threads from adjacent pairs of the first round, thus forming triangular spaces (diagram 32, figure 52).

Work the inner round of interlacing first as though it were a single round, using the pairs as grouped by the inner round of knot stitch. Work the outer round of knot stitch as before using the pairs as grouped by the outer round of knot stitch.

Diagram 32
Double rounds of interlacing

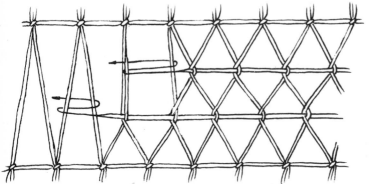

Figure 52
Double rounds of interlacing

Figure 53
The back section of the ñanduti
collar in figure 22 showing
interlacing

Figure 54
The side section of the ñanduti
collar in figure 22 showing
interlacing

Figure 55
The point of the ñanduti collar in
figure 22 showing interlacing

Looped and zigzag interlacing

Other forms of interlacing can be worked over a set of squares formed by rounds of knot stitch. Care must be taken not to distort this framework (diagrams 33 and 34, figures 56 and 57).

This stitch can be worked with the interlacing on one side only, the needle passing behind the web threads on the other (diagram 35, figure 56).

Diagram 33
Looped interlacing over squares

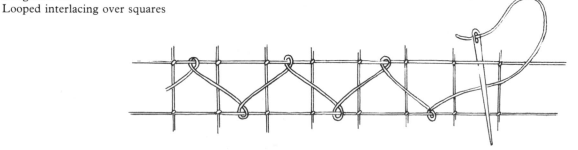

Diagram 34
Zigzag interlacing over squares

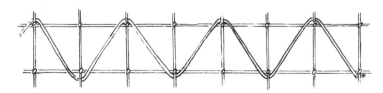

Figure 56
Two varieties of interlacing

Figure 57
Another variation on interlacing

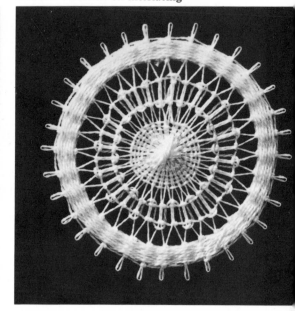

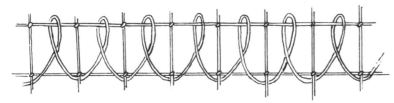

Diagram 35
Looped and zigzag
interlacing combined

Lace filling stitch

The lace filling stitch is a four-sided version of the looped interlacing
and can be worked in alternate (diagram 36) or adjacent squares
(diagram 37). When it is worked in alternate spaces the thread is
whipped along one of the rounds of knot stitch bounding the blank
space (figures 58 and 59)

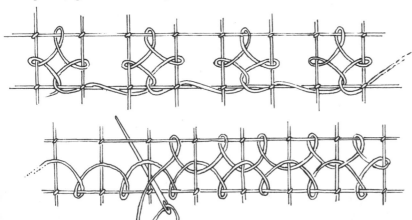
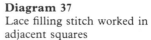

Diagram 36
Lace filling stitch worked in
alternate squares

Diagram 37
Lace filling stitch worked in
adjacent squares

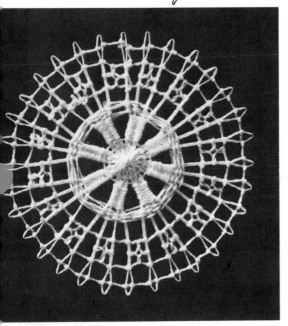

Figure 58
Lace filling stitch worked in
alternate squares

Figure 59
Lace filling stitch worked in
adjacent squares

ADDITIONAL EMBROIDERY

Whipping
A contrasting colour can be added by whipping over the rounds of knot stitch to form blocks, working either between the knot stitch rounds (diagram 38) or the web threads (diagram 39).

Diagram 38
Whipped blocks worked over knot stitch rounds

Diagram 39
Whipped blocks worked over the web threads

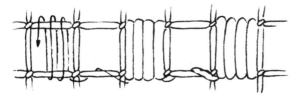

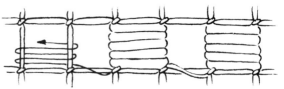

EDGINGS

The edge of the medallion is usually finished with a round of knot stitch.

Picot edge
The last round of knot stitch groups pairs of threads supported by the same pin (diagram 40, figure 46).

Scalloped edge
The last round of knot stitch groups the threads in pairs with one thread coming from each of two adjacent pairs (diagram 41, figure 60).

Diagram 40
A picot edge

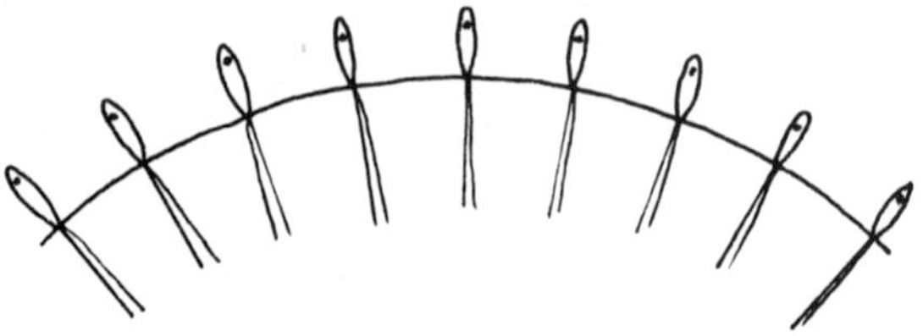

Diagram 41
A scalloped edge

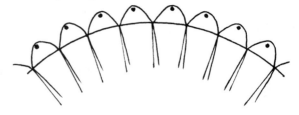

Looped edge
The last round knots each thread singly (diagram 42, figure 61).

Combination edge
The threads are grouped into fours with the centre two being supported by a single pin and the outer threads coming from the pins on either side (diagram 43, figure 43).

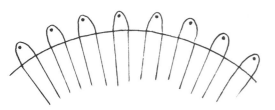

Diagram 42
A looped edge

Diagram 43
A combination edge

Figure 60
A scalloped edge

Figure 61
A looped edge

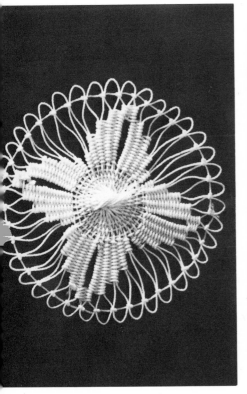

Plain edge

The last round has the knots worked outside the pins with one knot worked for each pair of threads (diagram 44, figure 62).

Buttonholed edge

See diagram 45 and figure 63. After the embroidery has been completed the working thread is taken two or more times around the circle of pins. Buttonhole stitch is then worked over these threads to form bars between the pins, with one or two stitches worked into each loop of the web supported by the pins (see diagram 45).

Diagram 44
A plain edge

Diagram 45
A buttonholed edge

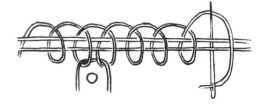

Figure 62
A plain edge

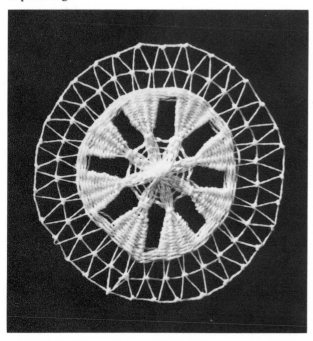

Figure 63
A buttonholed edge

CHAPTER 5

Constructing Plans

Most Teneriffe lace is worked using circles 2.5–10 cm (1–4 in) in diameter with 12 to 96 pins around the outer edge. The most usual sizes are 5–7.5 cm (2–3 in), with 32, 36, 40 or 48 pins. The plan is constructed by dividing a circle into the required number of sections using a protractor. The sections and circumference are drawn up on one sheet of paper, then the positions of the joins are transferred onto a second sheet of paper which becomes the working plan.

MAKING A MASTER PLAN

Dividing the circle accurately

There are 180° (degrees) in a semicircle. These are marked on protractors (available at most stationers) usually with every 10° marked with a heavy line. The plan in the example given is a circle 7.5 cm (3 in) in diameter with 32 pins round the circumference. As there are therefore 16 pins in the half circle, the 180° must be divided by 16; $180° \div 16 = 11\frac{1}{4}°$.

Before using the protractor, draw a straight line about 12.5 cm (5 in) across the centre of the paper and mark a dash across the centre of the line. Place the protractor on the paper so that the 0–180° line of the protractor covers the pencil line, and the 90° line of the protractor points to the dash on the pencil line (diagram 46).

The points can now be marked in at $11\frac{1}{4}°$ intervals around the protractor (guessing the $\frac{1}{4}°$). If a table is worked out beforehand the marking is easier:

1. mark $11\frac{1}{4}$
2. mark $22\frac{1}{2}$ ($2 \times 11\frac{1}{4}$)
3. mark $33\frac{3}{4}$ ($3 \times 11\frac{1}{4}$)
   etc.

When the first half of the circle has been marked the paper is turned round and the protractor positioned on the pencil line again so that

67

the remainder of the circle can be marked (diagram 47). Remember that accuracy is essential for good results.

Marking the radials and circumference
When the protractor has been removed, lines can be drawn using a pencil and straight edge connecting opposite points, thus producing 32 lines radiating from the centre (diagram 48). Take care to match the pencil marks up exactly before drawing the connecting line. Compasses are used to draw the circumference of the circle, which has a radius of 3.8 cm ($1\frac{1}{2}$ in).

Transferring the pin positions
Carbon paper is convenient for transferring the points (which will be the pin positions) to the notepaper. A stylus or ball-point pen is pressed on each of the points where the circle crosses the 32 lines and the central dot should also be marked (diagram 50).

Marking in the guidelines
Concentric circles can be drawn in as guidelines with a pair of compasses; these make it much easier to keep the embroidery central (diagram 51).

RE-USING PLANS

The master plan (diagram 49) can be kept and re-used many times for producing further plans of the same size. By drawing larger or smaller circles on the master plan, different sized plans can also be made, all having the same number of points.

The same plan can be used again and again for making the lace if it is not crumpled, but designs with interlacing, and some with regrouping using knot stitch, draw the web threads tighter than others and it may be necessary to construct a new plan for each medallion.

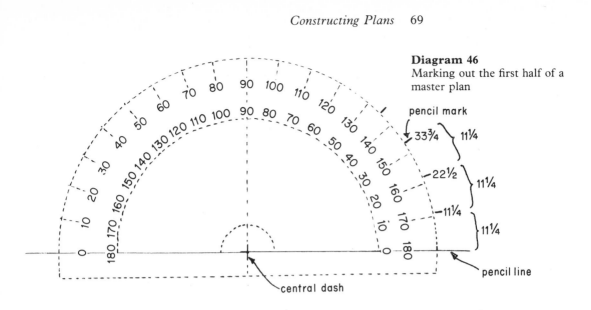

Diagram 46
Marking out the first half of a
master plan

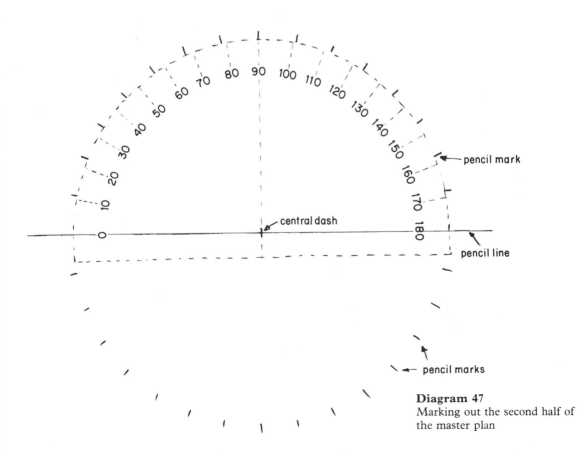

Diagram 47
Marking out the second half of
the master plan

Diagram 48
Drawing the radial lines on the
master plan

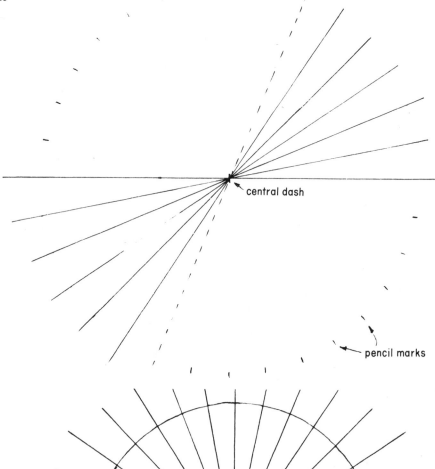

central dash

pencil marks

Diagram 49
Transferring the points to the
working plan

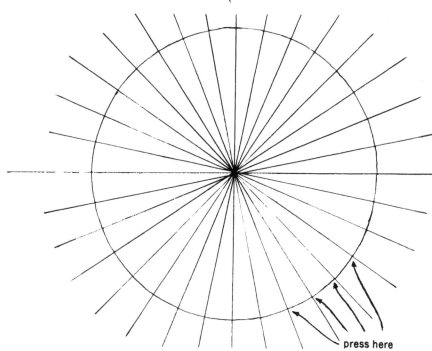

press here

central dot

The points of the plan marked in

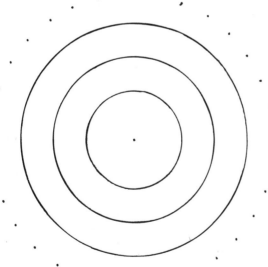

Diagram 51
A working plan with guidelines

CHAPTER 6

New Shapes and Different Webs

The circle, although the one most frequently worked, is not the only shape to be made using this technique. All the plans shown are suitable for tracing, but the guidelines have been omitted for simplicity.

SQUARES

Squares can be planned using the same master plan as for circles, since the lines connecting the points to the centre must be equally spaced; the corners may be placed on the lines (diagram 52, figure 64) or in the spaces (diagram 53, figure 65). This may make the plan look odd but the final effect will be better than it would be if the

Diagram 52
A plan for a square medallion with pins at the corners

Figure 64
A square medallion with pins at the corners of the plan

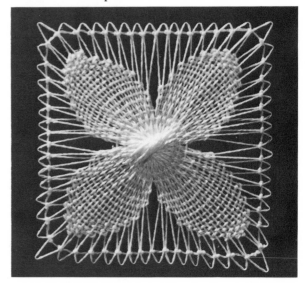

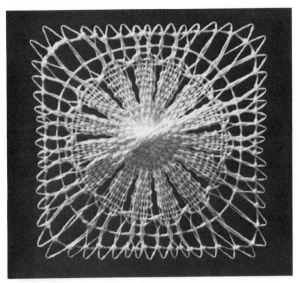

Figure 65
A square medallion with the
corners situated between pins on
the plan

Diagram 53
A plan for a square medallion
with the corners situated between
the pins

points were equally spaced. Care must be taken to keep the design
and the edging symmetrical.

SHIELDS

These are also planned on the master plan used for circles, and take
the form of one half circle, one half square (diagram 54, figure 66).
Again, keep the design and edging as symmetrical as possible.

Figure 66
A shield shaped medallion

Diagram 54
A plan for a shield shaped
medallion

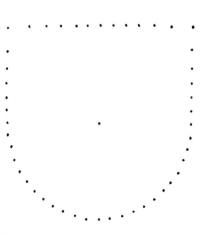

Figure 67
Shield shaped medallions forming
a scalloped border

Similar medallions joined in a row produce a scalloped edging
(diagram 55, figure 67).

Diagram 55
Joining shields to make a
scalloped edging

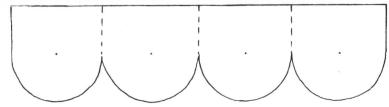

PEAR SHAPES

Circles extending into a point on one side can be easily linked
together to form small mats. The shape of each section is determined by dividing a circle into the required number of sections
using a protractor, and placing a suitable circle in one of the sections
so that it just touches the line on each side (diagram 56).
The circle is now traced around and the section of circle and point
cut out. Now place it on the master plan (use a pin through the
centre of the circle to locate the centre of the master plan), with the
point coinciding with one of the lines or centre of a space, and trace
round. The points along the boundary can be transferred to a piece
of plain paper using carbon paper (diagram 57, figure 69).

Figure 68
Six pear shaped medallions joined
to form a mat

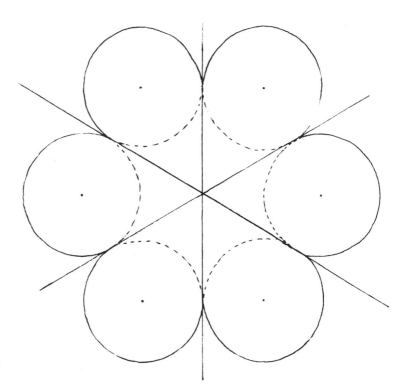

Diagram 56
Six pear shaped medallions joined
to form a mat

Figure 69
A pear shaped medallion

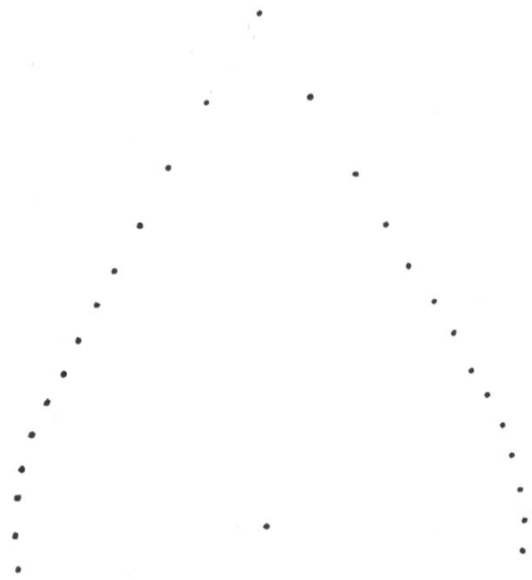

Diagram 57
A plan for a pear shaped
medallion

STAR CENTRES

Very attractive mats can be made using four or more circular medallions with a centre tailored to fit (diagram 58, figure 70). To design such a centre the circular plans are fitted onto a master plan with twice the number of radial lines as used for the circles themselves. The inner curves of the circles are traced round and the plan made as usual. In practice the centre may require modifying. This depends on the stitches used to decorate the pieces, and how much of the work entails regrouping in knot stitch and interlacing,

Figure 70
A traditional Teneriffe design

Diagram 58
A star centre

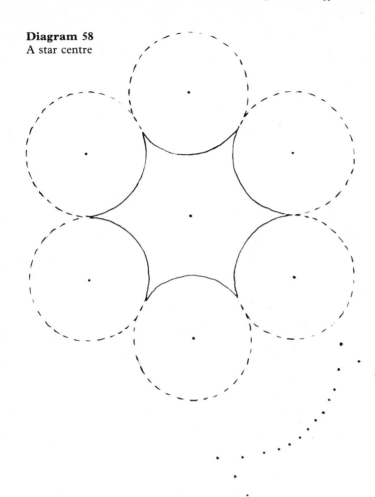

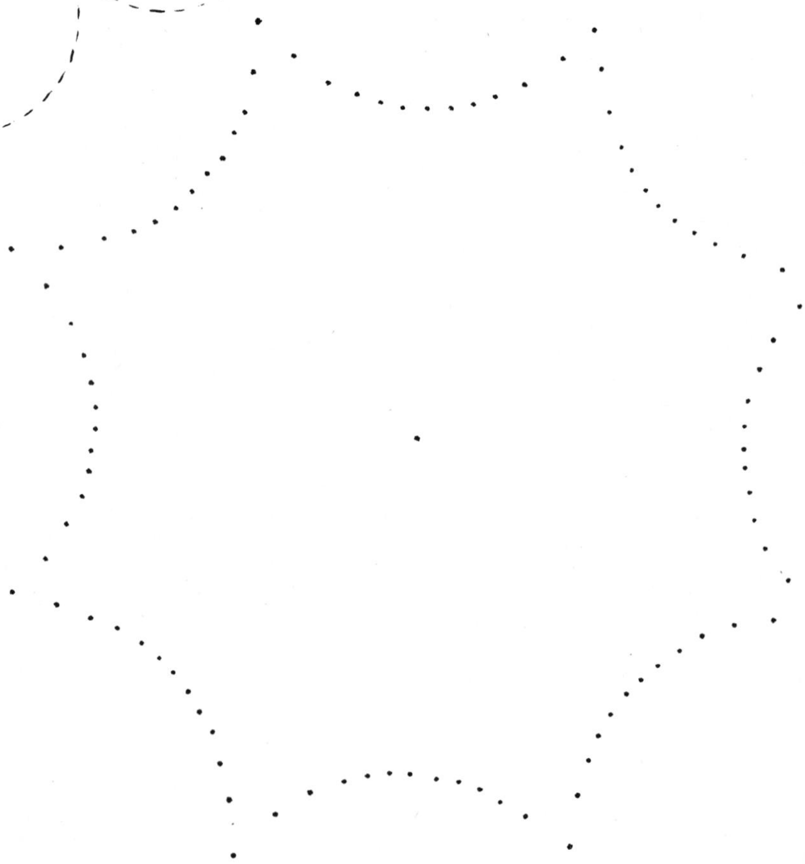

Diagram 59
A plan for a star centre

Diagram 60
A plan for an accompanying
circular medallion

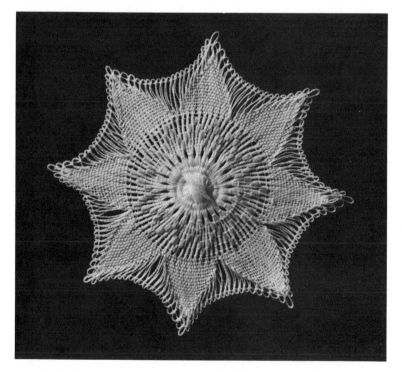

Figure 71
A star centre

both of which modify the size of the finished article (diagrams 59
and 60, figure 71). The points of the star may also require
shortening. The embroidery of the star centre should imitate or
complement the design of the medallions. The different parts are
assembled with an oversewing stitch.

All the shapes described above have their webs stretched as for the circle. The embroidery can be worked either following the outline or as for the circular medallion with the added space worked afterwards. The following designs are not only new shapes, they have different webs also.

Figure 72
A doily edging

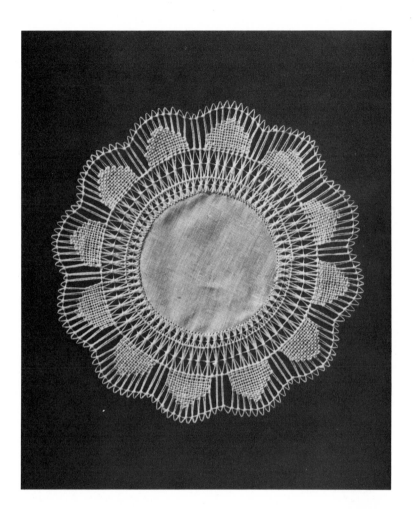

DOILY EDGING

The plan is marked out using the circle master plan. The outer edge is circular and usually scalloped, the inner edge is also circular and has the same number of pins (diagram 61, figure 72). The web is stretched zigzag fashion between these two circles of pins, starting from inside the circle (diagram 62). When it has passed around the last pin (inner circle) the first round of knot stitch starts on the first web thread laid.

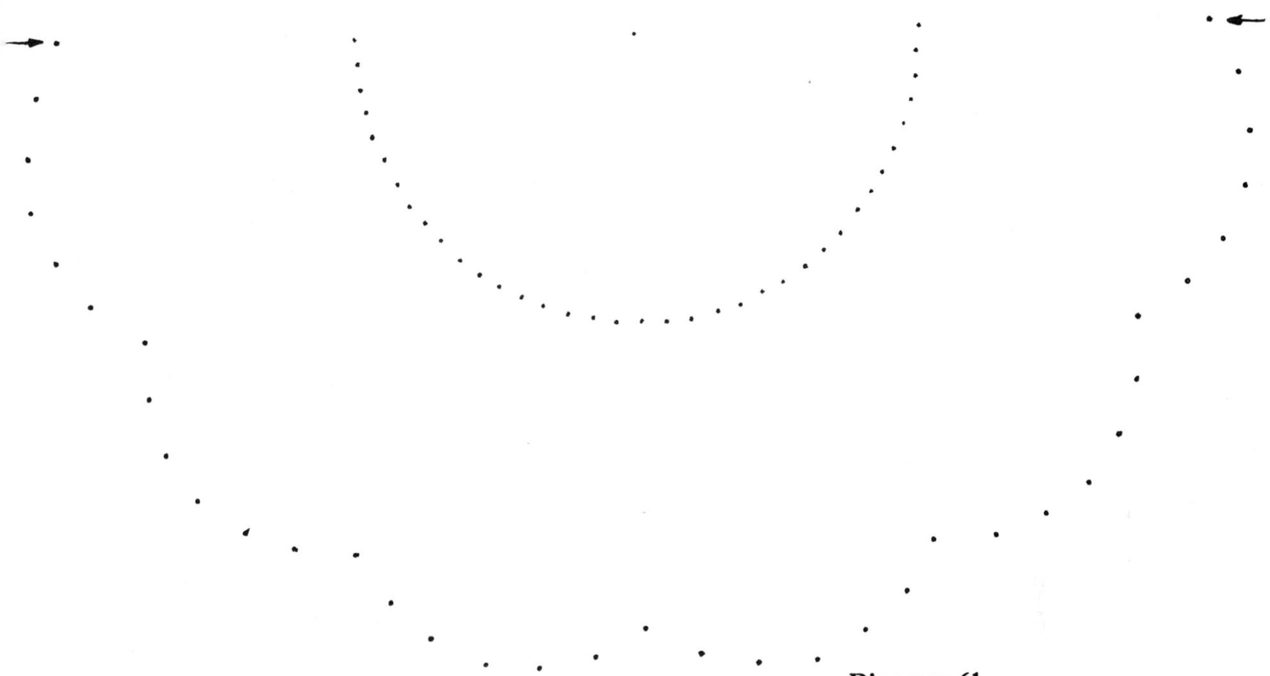

Diagram 61
A half plan for a doily edging (copy twice and tape the two pieces together before using)

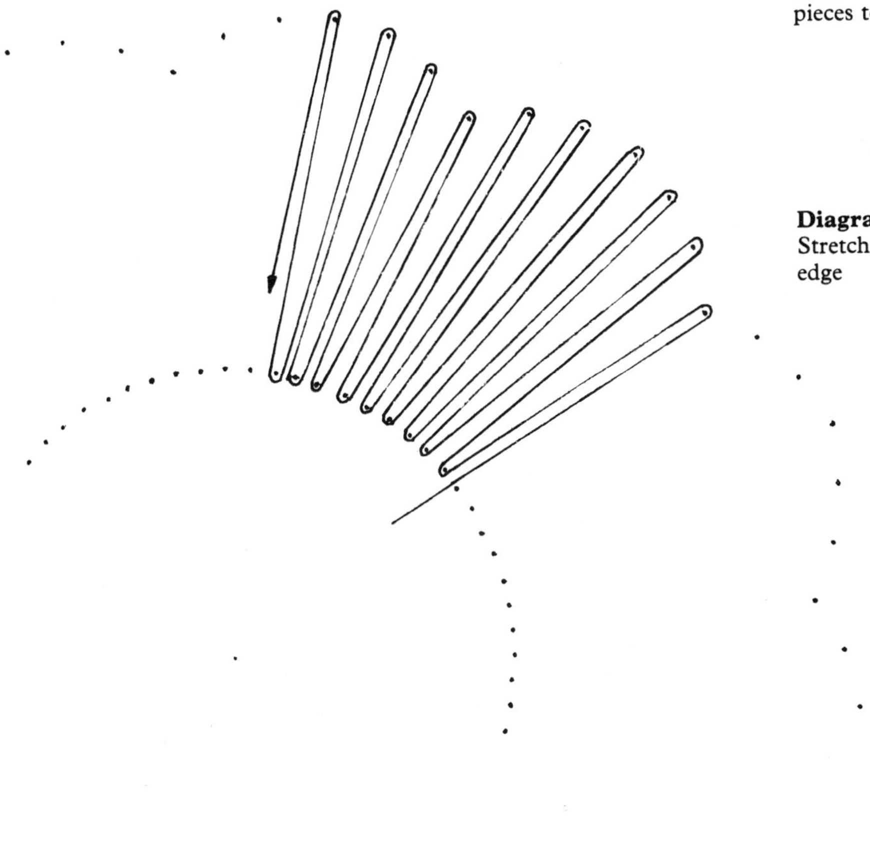

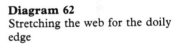

Diagram 62
Stretching the web for the doily edge

DOUBLE CIRCLES OF PINS

.When a medallion has a large number of pins around the edge, the proportionately large number of threads crossing at the centre forms a thick lump. This is one of the characteristics of this lace and part of the design. However, the thickness can be reduced, if desired, by introducing a small inner circle having half as many pins as the outer one (diagram 63, figure 73).

The web is stretched in two layers. The first layer is stretched as for the Doily Edging, passing round the pins of the inner circle and alternate pins of the outer circle (diagram 64). The second layer is stretched across the remaining pins in the usual manner. The centre is darned as usual and the embroidery must contain a round of knot stitch just outside the inner ring of pins, joining the two webs together.

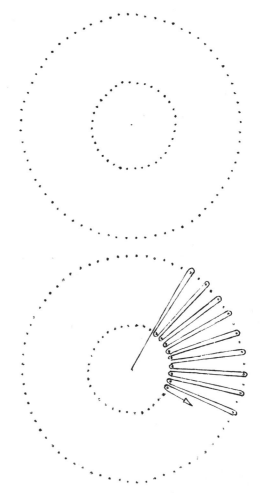

Diagram 63
A plan for a medallion using two circles of pins

Diagram 64
The first stage in stretching the web over two circles of pins

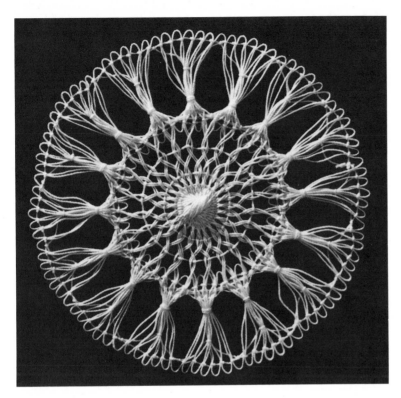

Figure 73
A medallion with the web
stretched over two circles of pins

SMALL CIRCLES

Very small circles of 2.5 cm (1 in) diameter and smaller can be made
with holes in the centre by stretching the web in a different manner.
For example, for a 2 cm ($\frac{3}{4}$ in) diameter medallion with 20 points
(diagram 65, figure 74), number the points on the plan 1 to 20.
Stretch the web by bringing the thread from outside between 20
and 1 around the pins in the following order: 9, 18, 7, 16, 5, 14, 3,
12, 1, 10, 19, 8, 17, 6, 15, 4, 13, 2, 11, 20 (diagram 66). Each time the
pin used is the one before the opposite. This results in a web which

Diagram 66
Stretching the web for a small
medallion with a hole in the
centre

Diagram 65
A plan for a small medallion

Figure 74
A small circular medallion with a
hole in the centre

separates in the centre to form a hole. The edges of the hole are
bound in oversewing, with the thread passing round the group of
threads encircling the centre and passing up through the space
made by each pin in turn. This thread is fastened off by passing it
through the group of threads encircling the centre. The remainder
of the medallion may be decorated or simply have a single round of
knot stitch to form the outer edge.

OVALS, LEAVES AND CRESCENTS

The plans for these shapes cannot be made by using the circle
master plan, as the mathematics would be exceptionally difficult.
The best way is to put the points in 'by eye'. The outline of the
shape should be drawn first keeping 'points' rather blunt. A 'centre'
should then be drawn near each end; for the rounded end of an oval
or leaf the 'centre' will be about half the width of the shape at that
point from the end, and for the pointed end of the leaf or crescent
about the width of the shape at that point from the end. However,
these measurements are only guides and are better judged by eye
rather than measured, as is the spacing of the points around the edge
(diagrams 67, 68 and 69, figures 75, 76 and 77).

The stretching of the web should be considered when marking
the points as it follows a different pattern. The web is started by
taking the thread through one of the 'centres' and knotting. The pin
is then replaced. The web is formed by following the sequence
marked on the example with the thread passing between the two
'centres' each time it travels from one pin to the one with the next
number. When one end has been completed the thread zigzags
across the shape until the next 'centre' is encountered when a

Diagram 67
A plan for an oval medallion

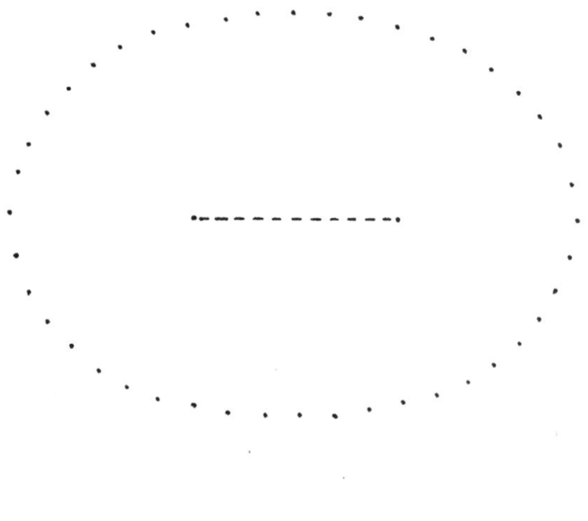

Figure 75
An oval medallion

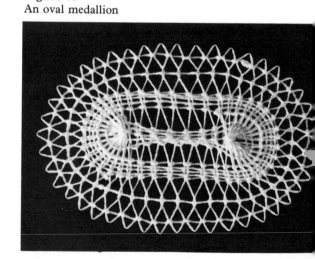

pattern, similar to that of the first end, is worked (diagram 70).

The embroidery commences with a line of knot stitch starting at the 'centre' where the web was finished. This line of stitching travels along the central line of the shape that links the two. The rest of the web can be decorated as usual.

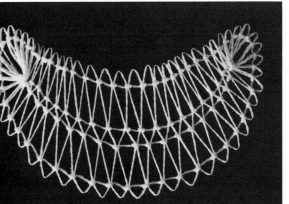

Figure 76
A crescent shaped medallion

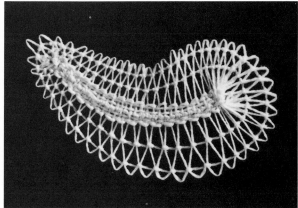

Figure 77
A leaf shaped medallion

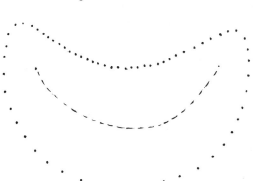

Diagram 68
A plan for a crescent shaped
medallion

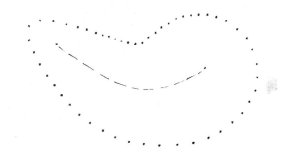

Diagram 69
A plan for a leaf shaped
medallion

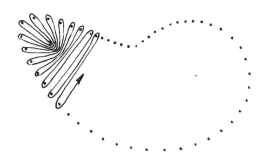

Diagram 70
Stretching the web at the pointed
end of the leaf

STRAIGHT EDGING

Edgings and insertions may be worked on the straight by laying down a zigzag web across two straight lines of pins (diagrams 71 and 72, figure 78). The straight lines can be drawn with equal divisions simply using a ruler; the dots should be staggered to allow the thread to zigzag between them.

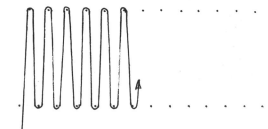

Diagram 71
A plan for an edging or insertion

Diagram 72
Stretching the web for an edging

Figure 78
An edging

SCALLOPED EDGING

If two lines of dots are drawn and one of the lines undulates, a scalloped edging is produced (diagram 73, figure 79). Use a ruler and pencil to draw and mark off the divisions of the straight line. Then draw a further two lines which will give the top and bottom limits of the scallops. Design the shape of one half of a scallop, ensuring that the dots correspond to those along the straight edge, then place a piece of tracing paper over the half scallop and mark the positions of the dots. Use this tracing to repeat the half scallop shape all the way along the undulating edge. The tracing can be used with the paper one side up for one half of the scallop and turned over for the other half. Prick through each dot with a pin.

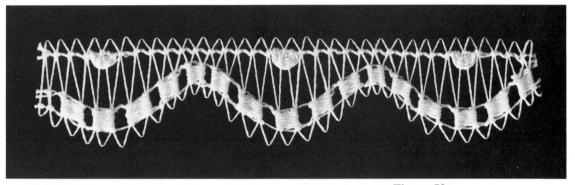

Diagram 73
A plan for a scalloped edging

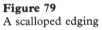

FRINGING

Figure 79
A scalloped edging

If the lines are widely spaced and the embroidery worked along one side only, then the loops along the other side can be clipped making a fringe (diagram 74, figure 80).

Figure 80
A fringe

Diagram 74
Stretching the web
for a fringe

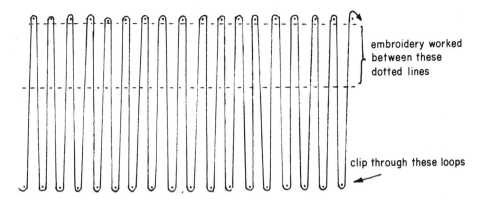

embroidery worked
between these
dotted lines

clip through these loops

Diagram 75a
A plan for a large medallion
surrounded by shell
shapes

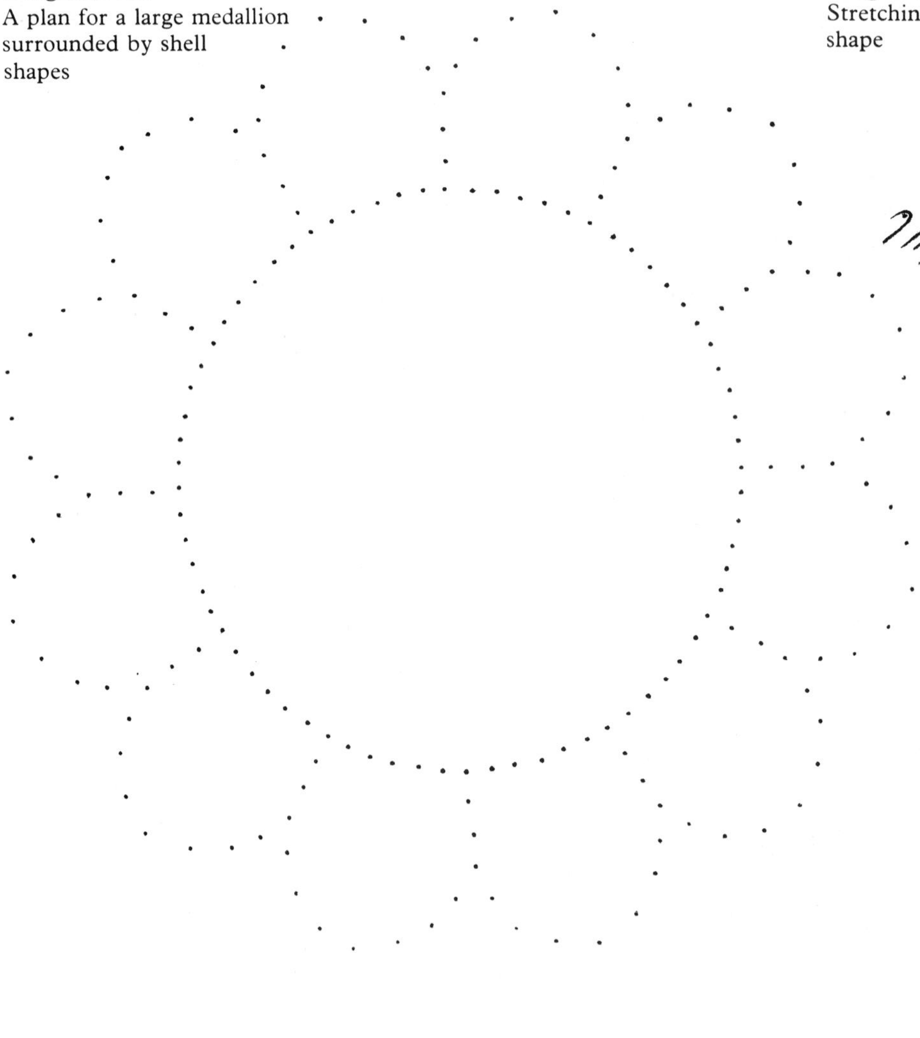

Diagram 75b
Stretching the web for a shell
shape

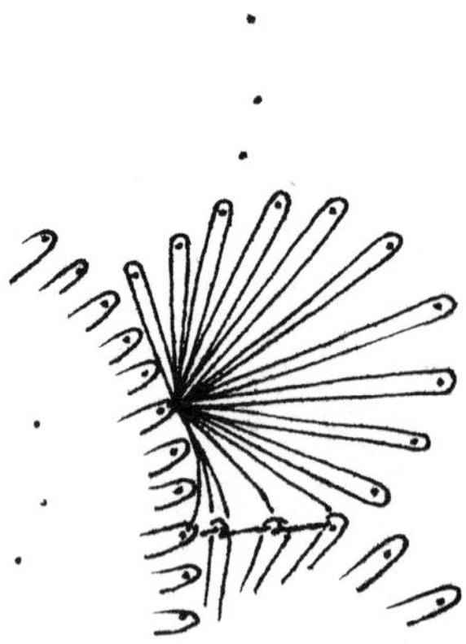

SHELL SHAPES

This shape is typical of Paraguayan work and is usually worked into the edge of a piece of work, not as a separate piece to be sewn on after it is made. Such shells have been used to surround the central motif of the Paraguayan tablecloth (figure 16), and the smaller circular motifs (figure 20) and the collars (figures 21 and 22).

The motif reaching the straight edge of the shell must be completed first. Then the web of the shell can be stretched by passing the thread through the central spoke of the motif meeting its straight edge, round the pin nearest the motif on one side, through the central spoke again, round the next pin and so on until the thread reaches the central spoke for the last time. (Always pass the needle through the central spoke the same way.) The darning starts by taking the thread through the next spoke of the motif; it then works through the web of the shell to the spoke of the motif on the other side of the centre (diagrams 75a and b). The remaining spokes of the motif bounding the straight side are anchored by supporting lines of knot stitch.

When the web of the next shell is laid the spokes should interlock with the first by passing the web thread of the second through two adjacent spokes of the first before passing it back across (figure 81).

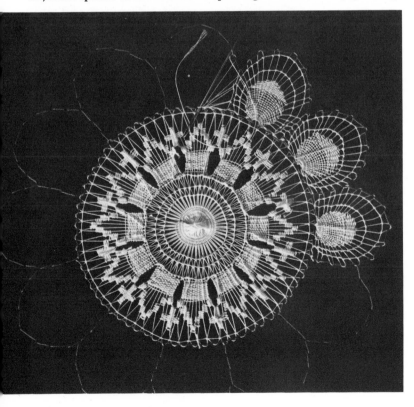

Figure 81
A large medallion surrounded by shell shapes

SPIDERS

A spider is used to fill spaces between medallions. When the medallions have been joined together, the web is stretched between seven of the eight loops in order (diagram 76), then the thread is passed across the centre and used to work two or more rounds of darning. After anchoring the thread in the usual way, it is taken through the eighth loop to make the last 'leg' (figure 82).

Diagram 76
Stretching the web and starting the darning for a spider filling

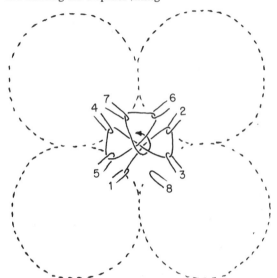

Figure 82
A spider filling

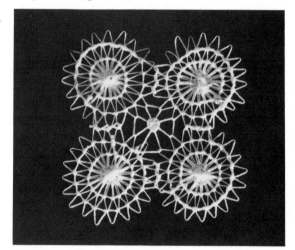

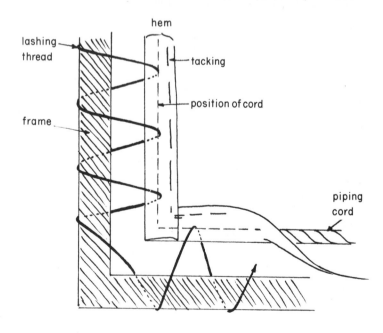

Diagram 77
Lashing the linen to the frame (see page 96)

WORKING LARGER UNITS

The Paraguayan collar in figure 22 contains examples of techniques needed when working larger units (figures 83 to 87).

Figure 83
The back section of the ñanduti
collar in figure 21 showing the
fillings

Figure 84
The left side section of the
ñanduti collar in figure 21
showing the fillings

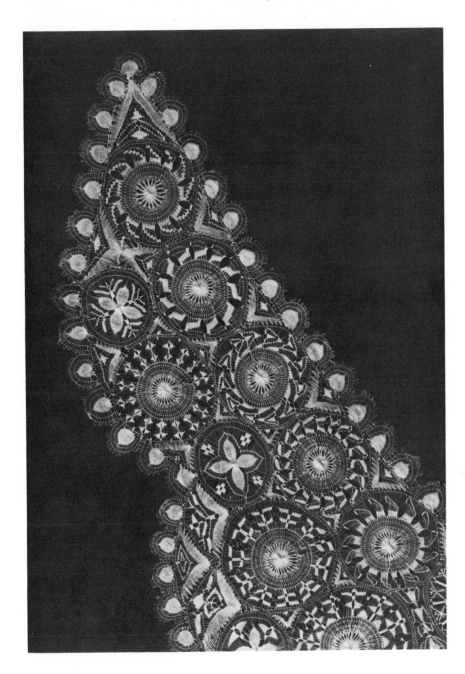

Figure 85
The left point of the ñanduti
collar in figure 21 showing the
fillings

Figure 86
The right side section of the
ñanduti collar in figure 21
showing the fillings

Figure 87
The right point of the ñanduti
collar in figure 21 showing the
fillings

When a large piece is being made, it is usually easier to make it in the same manner as the Sol laces, supporting the web on a double line of running stitches set in linen (or any strong fabric) mounted in a frame such as an embroidery frame. (See chapter 9.) The frame can be constructed in any way which will hold the fabric taut. A simple method is to tack a 2 cm ($\frac{3}{4}$ in) hem, containing parcel string or no. 2 piping cord around the edge of the linen to strengthen it (diagram 77, page 90) and lash it to a square wooden frame which is slightly larger than the fabric.

The design is drawn on paper and transferred to the linen using the special type of carbon paper which is produced for use with fabrics. A double line of running stitches is worked along all the lines, and the web is stretched using the stitches instead of pins (see chapter 9). Each medallion is completed in turn with the webs interlocked where they touch (diagram 78, figure 88). To release the lace, the running stitches are cut on the other side of the fabric to ensure that the scissors do not damage the completed work.

Diagram 78
Interlocking the webs

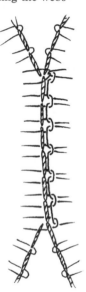

Figure 88
Interlocking two webs

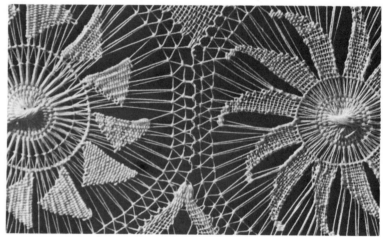

FILLING A SPACE

A triangle of darning can be used to fill an odd space between medallions (diagram 79, figure 89). After all the surrounding medallions have been completed, the web is stretched from one corner and interlocked with the other side. The darning is started at the corner where all the web threads meet and passes from the spoke of the medallion on one side to the spoke of the medallion on the other side. The thread may pass through each of these spokes more than once to make a neat piece of darning. This motif has been used in the Paraguayan tablecloth shown in figures 17 and 18.

1 Teneriffe lace mats and medallions used in a tray, compact, brooch, paperweight, ash tray and trinket boxes

2 Teneriffe lace used to decorate a
dress, pendant, brooch and bag; a
butterfly motif has been used in the
round picture frame

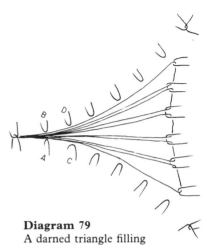

Figure 89
A darned triangular filling

Diagram 79
A darned triangle filling

FILLING A TRIANGLE

When one side of a triangle is longer than the others, the web should be stretched from this one to the opposite corner. After the first few lines of darning, the web threads are divided in two and each side darned separately, leaving out threads from the centre after each row, and using the loops of the medallions at the sides at least once each to anchor them. The floating threads in the centre may need a little embroidery to keep them tidy (diagram 80, figure 90).

Diagram 80
A second darned triangle filling

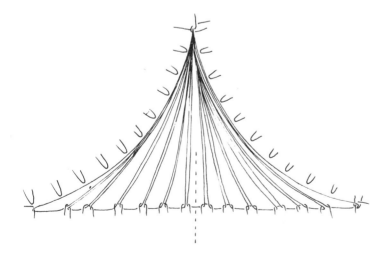

Figure 90
An alternative filling for a
triangular space

CHEQUERED FILLINGS

Large irregular spaces can be filled with chequered fillings. After
the surrounding medallions have been completed, a web is
stretched having one set of threads lying parallel to each other
(diagram 81), a second set lying at right angles to these (diagram 82)
and another forming the diagonals of the squares so formed
(diagram 83). As the diagonals are stretched, knots must be worked
where one diagonal crosses another. The intersections where eight
threads meet are centres for embroidery. The simplest filling is a
mixture of spiders and windmills of four darned triangles (diagram
84, figure 91).

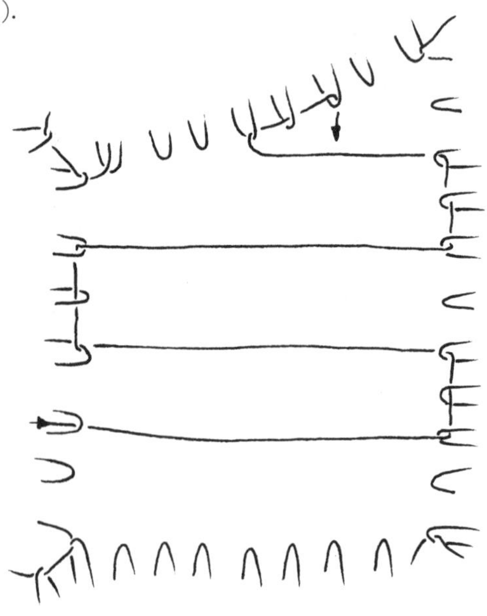

Diagram 81
The first stage in stretching the
web for a chequered filling

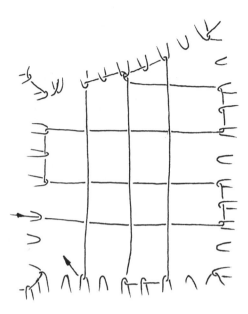

Diagram 82
The second stage in stretching the
web for a chequered filling

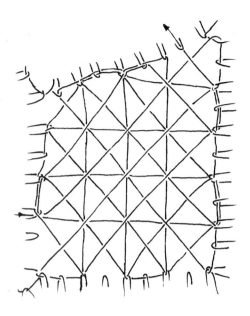

Diagram 83
The last stage in stretching the
web for a chequered filling

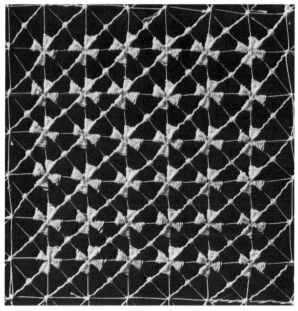

Figure 91
A chequered filling

Diagram 84
A typical chequered filling of
darned triangles and spiders

CHAPTER 7

Modern Developments in Teneriffe Lace

Handcrafts never, or should never, remain static. New techniques and materials will appear from time to time and fashion create a new emphasis. Thus the craft evolves. At the same time, the best of the old techniques and patterns are kept alive and the subject develops. Since the turn of the century Teneriffe lace has grown a new branch. The emphasis switches from the embroidery, and the pattern of the web resulting from the embroidery, to the loops of the web themselves. In many cases the medallions, or 'flowers' as they are called, are joined to make a fabric for a garment such as a blouse or shawl; in others they are made to be used on their own. This branch has become commercialised and manufactured wheels are available for stretching the web.

THE DAISY WINDER

The first to be produced was at about the turn of the century and was a metal disc some 5 cm (2 in) across with twelve spokes that could be removed or retracted. A web of wool or cotton is stretched across the disc with two or more loops supported by each spoke. The centre of the flower is worked in stem stitch and the flower set free by removing or retracting the spokes of the wheel. The flowers can be joined by using crochet to form attractive garments, pram covers and other articles (see figures 92, 93 and colour plate 4).

Making daisies on the daisy winder
Turn the knob at the back of the winder to extend the spokes. Tie the end of the thread to the knob and start stretching the web as for Teneriffe lace (diagram 85). If only one loop is made round each spoke the final result may be rather thin and spidery, so, after completing the web with one loop per spoke, repeat the stretching of the web until there are two loops round each spoke. Cut the thread leaving a 25 cm (10 in) length for working the centre. Using a tapestry needle pass the thread between two petals and under four

Figure 92
Three daisy winders

Figure 93
A motif worked on the daisy
winder

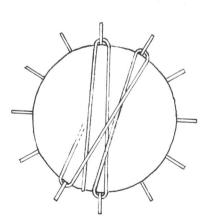

Diagram 85
Stretching the web on a daisy
winder

towards the left. Draw the thread through tightly. Take the needle over the first three petals to the right, then under these and the next one on the left. Keep working back over three and under four until thirteen stitches have been worked (diagram 86). Fasten off by sewing the thread through the centre, first one way and then the other. Cut the knot, anchoring the thread to the knob. This may also be fastened off by sewing it through the centre. If the thread is too short for the needle, pass the needle part way through the centre before threading. Trim off all the ends. The daisies may be used singly or joined with crochet (see colour plate 4).

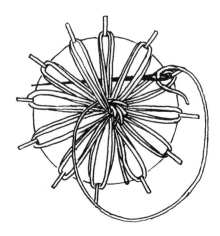

Diagram 86
Working the centre of a daisy

Pattern for joining the daisies
This pattern may be used for pram covers, jumpers, cushion covers, etc.

Abbreviations

ss – slip stitch	dc – double crochet
ch – chain	p – picot, worked 5 ch, ss into side of last dc

First daisy:　ss into one petal, *(4 ch, dc into next petal) 3 times, p; repeat from * working last dc into first ss, fasten off.

Second daisy:　ss into one petal, (4 ch, dc into next petal) 3 times, 2 ch, ss into centre ch of p of first daisy, 2 ch, ss into last dc (joined to p of first daisy), (2 ch, dc into 4 ch of first daisy, 2 ch, dc into next petal) 5 times, join to p of first daisy. Complete second daisy as first.

Continuing the pattern:　continue joining the daisies as required. As more rows are added the daisies will require joining by two sides instead of only one.

THE MULTI-NEEDLE

The next change came with the appearance of the multi-needle in the mid 1960s. This makes similar flowers but an attachment that fits on the round wheel enables squares and diamond shapes to be made as well as the more usual circular flower. A different method of working the centre of the flower is recommended and this results in a hole instead of a knob at the centre. A line of knot stitch is worked around the outside of the spokes to keep the petals in place. This outer line of stitching can also be used to link the flowers together, a useful method for those who dislike or who are unable to crochet (see figures 94 and 95, and colour plate 4).

Figure 94
A multi-needle with retractable spokes, an adapter and a square motif being worked

Figure 95
A wedding dress of multi-needle
motifs (courtesy of Carter and
Parker Ltd)

Making rosettes on the multi-needle
Turn the knob at the end of the handle of the multi-needle to extend the spokes. Make a slip knot about 45 cm (18 in) from the end of the thread, if a knot stitch edge is to be worked, and tighten around the handle. Start stretching the web as for Teneriffe lace (diagram 87) until all the prongs have been looped, continue round until all have been looped twice, then cut the thread allowing 25 cm (10 in) for making the centre. Using a tapestry needle, form the centre by passing the needle under the threads from the centre and out between two petals. *Pass the needle under the threads from the centre so that it comes out between the next two petals. Repeat from * until thirteen stitches have been made (diagram 88).

Work one more oversew stitch, making a knot to secure the thread. Pull up tightly and pass the needle through the thickness of the ring of oversewing to fasten off. Cut the thread off closely.

Diagram 87
Stretching the web on a multi-needle

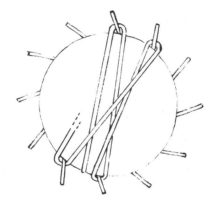

Figure 96
A circular motif made on the multi-needle

Diagram 88
Oversewing the centre of a rosette

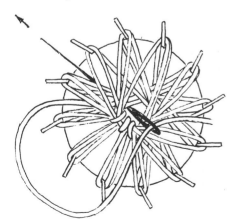

Knot stitch edging

With the rosette still on the multi-needle, loosen and remove the slip knot from the handle and use this thread to work the edging. Using a tapestry needle, sew upwards on the left side of the prong. (diagram 89). Sew upwards a second time through the same petal and, while the loop is still open, make a knot by passing the needle from right to left through this loop (diagram 90). Close the loop by pulling down sharply, tightening the knot below the prong. Continue round the rosette leaving the thread between the knots a little loose to prevent distortion. (Check after making the first rosette.) After making the last knot over the first, take the thread across to the oversewn ring, and fasten off by passing the needle through the thickness of the ring. Cut off the remaining thread, and release by turning the knob at the end of the handle.

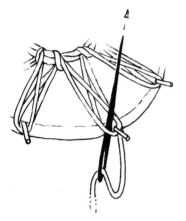

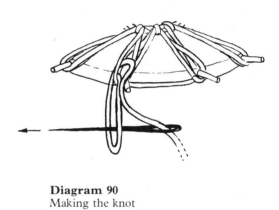

Diagram 90
Making the knot

Diagram 89
A knot stitch edging for a rosette

Pearl or rhinestone studded centre

Allow 30 cm (12 in) for oversewing the centre. Complete the oversewing of the centre by passing the needle through the oversewn ring to the open centre. Thread on the pearl or rhinestone, a needle threader may be the best way, and sew outwards through the other side of the oversewn ring (diagram 91). Make another oversew stitch where the needle comes out, drawing the needle through the loop to secure it. Pass the needle through the thickness of the ring and cut off the surplus thread.

Joining round rosettes

Make one rosette, and remove it from the multi-needle. Stretch the web of the second rosette and oversew the centre. Leaving the unfinished rosette on the multi-needle, place the complete one wrong side up on top, looping two petals of the complete rosette round the first two prongs where the knot stitch edging is to start.

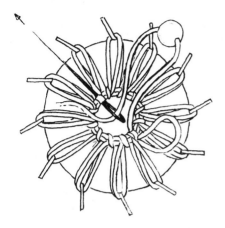

Diagram 91
Adding a pearl or rhinestone to a
rosette

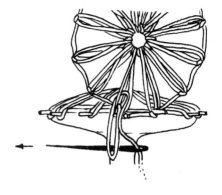

Diagram 92
Joining rosettes with knot stitch

Work the first two knots through the petals of both rosettes, so
securing them together (diagram 92). Once two pairs of petals have
been joined, lift off the top rosette and complete the knot stitch
edging round the unfinished rosette only, and remove it from the
multi-needle. The two rosettes will be joined by two petals. A third
rosette is joined to the second similarly. If a strip is being made,
ensure that subsequent rosettes are joined to opposite petals. After
completing the first strip each rosette must be joined to both
adjacent rosettes (diagram 93) by working the knot stitch round first
with one rosette on top, then replacing this with the other. As each
rosette is released it is completely attached to the article.

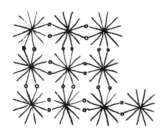

Diagram 93
Joining round rosettes (the circles
indicate petals joined by a knot)

Square rosettes

With the adapter in place on the multi-needle, stretch the web with the thread lying across the opening of each post, oversew the centre and work the knot stitch around the edge allowing a little more thread between the knots (diagram 94 and figure 97).

Figure 97
A square motif made on the
multi-needle

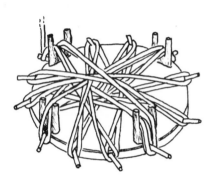

Diagram 94
Making square rosettes

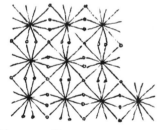

Diagram 95
Joining square rosettes (the circles
indicate petals joined by a knot)

Joining square rosettes

Follow the instructions for joining the round rosettes, but join four petals of the complete rosette to four of the incomplete one, starting at one post of the adapter and joining to the corner of the complete one, joining the petals at the next two prongs, and finishing by joining both rosettes at the next post. Lift off the complete rosette and finish the knot stitch edging of the other (diagram 95).

Diamond rosettes

Place the adapter on the multi-needle. Stretch the web as for the other rosettes, taking it across the opening of two opposite posts but around the other two opposite posts. Work the centre and the edge as before and stretch gently to shape after releasing (figure 98). Diamonds will retain their shape when joined together. Join as for the square rosettes.

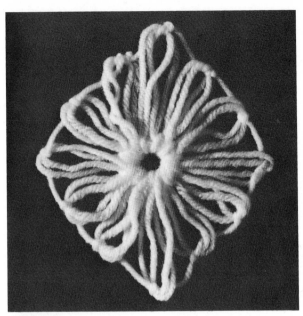

Figure 98
A diamond shaped motif made on
the multi-needle

THE FLOWER LOOM

The most recent development in the line of commercial wheels is
the flower loom (figures 99 and 100). This is a plastic disc with two
or more concentric circles of pegs protruding from it. Again the
charm and variety of the flowers formed depends on the winding of
the web and the colours used. A square loom is also produced, thus
increasing the number of variations. Flowers made on these looms
can be joined, usually by crochet, and used for items such as
bedspreads and waistcoats. Other materials are also very effective,
and raffia flowers make delightful Christmas decorations.

   When raffia (the plastic type) is used, the appearance of the flower
is determined by the pegs and combinations of pegs used, since
plastic raffia will hold a shape whereas wool and cotton will not.

Making a flower

Fasten the thread to the back of the loom using clear adhesive tape.
Start by stretching the web around the outer pegs (diagram 96) as
for Teneriffe lace, working round the loom three times so that there
are three loops round each peg. If a contrasting colour is to be used
for the smaller petals take the end of the thread across the loom and
fasten to the back with adhesive tape. If the first colour is to be used

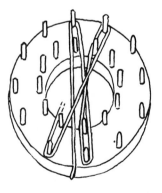

Diagram 96
Stretching the web across the
outer pegs of a flower loom

Figure 99
A circular flower loom

Figure 100
A square flower loom

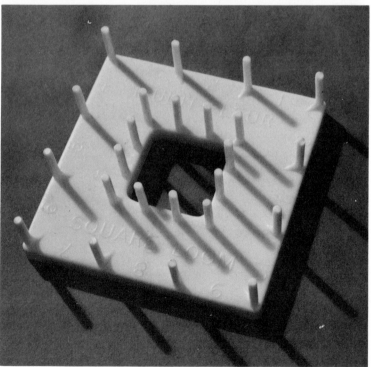

for fastening the centre, cut off the remaining thread allowing 40 cm (15 in).

Fasten the end of the contrasting thread to the back of the loom, or continue with the former thread, stretching it across the inner pegs only (diagram 97), and work round three times so that there are three loops per peg. If this colour is not to be used for stitching the centre take it across the centre and fasten at the back with adhesive tape, otherwise cut off leaving 40 cm (15 in) for the centre.

Using a tapestry needle, take the thread across the centre and down between two petals; bring it back up between two petals opposite. Back stitch the centre by taking the needle over one petal and back under that one and one more, over that one and under it again and one more; repeat until thirteen stitches have been worked. Fasten off by passing the needle through the centre first one way and then the other. Ease the flower off the loom and trim off the ends (figures 101 and 102).

Flower loom work is best done with the loom placed on a table. As the pegs fill up there is a tendency for the loops to slip off, so keep your left index finger in the centre holding the threads down, only raising it slightly to allow each new thread to pass across.

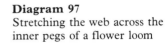

Diagram 97
Stretching the web across the inner pegs of a flower loom

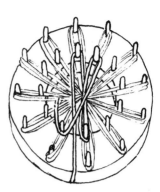

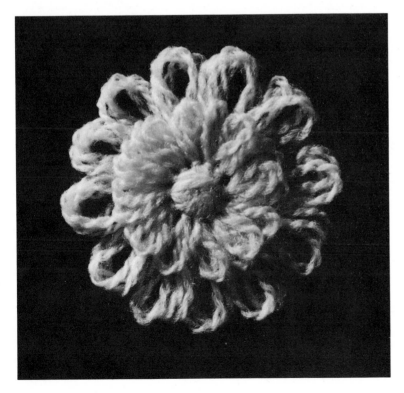

Figure 101
A motif made on the circular flower loom

Figure 102
A motif made on the square
flower loom

Joining flowers
Diagram 98 shows the order of work when using crochet to join the
flowers for pram covers, afghans, etc (as illustrated in colour plate 4).

Abbreviations
    ss – slip stitch
    ch – chain
    dc – double crochet
    joining – slip the loop off the hook, pass the hook through the dc
    of the other petal, pick up the original loop and pull through

Row 1:   Join the thread to any petal with a ss, (5 ch, dc into the next
petal) 7 times; *attach the next flower by working a dc into any
petal, 5 ch, dc into petal 2, join to petal 7 of the previous flower; (5
ch, dc into the next petal) 6 times. Repeat from * to the end of the

row.** (5 ch, dc into the next petal) 4 times; (5 ch, dc into the join between petals 1 and 8). Repeat from ** to the end of the row finishing with a ss into the first dc.

Row 2: Join to any petal of an unused flower with a ss; (5 ch, dc into next petal) twice. Join to petal 10 of the first flower of row 1; 5 ch, dc into petal 4, join to petal 9 of the first flower of row 1, 5 ch, dc into petal 5, join to petal 12 of the second flower of row 1, 5 dc, dc into petal 6, join to petal 11 of the second flower of row 1, (5 ch, dc into the next petal) twice, dc into any petal of an unused flower.

Work the rest of the row similarly joining the petals 2–6 to the previous row. At the end of the row continue round the flower and work along the other sides of the flowers as for row 1.

Row 3: Work as for row 2, but do not join petals 3 and 4 to the previous row.

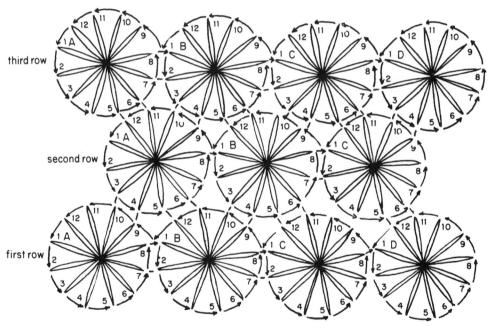

Diagram 98
Joining flowers with crochet
(work from the right side)

Stem stitched centre

When synthetic raffia is used the centre can be enhanced by working a heavier centre in stem stitch. After the normal back stitch centre has been worked, pass the needle under three petals to the right, * then back over two petals to the left, under both of those and the next on the right. Repeat from * all round. The final two stitches should be worked under the first two stem stitches made. Fasten off by passing the needle through the centre. Remove from the loom and trim off the ends (figure 103).

An alternative centre can be worked by passing the needle through the centres of the petals instead of the spaces between them (figure 104).

Figure 103
A flower with the long petals clipped and shredded and a stem stitched centre

Figure 104
A basic flower with a stem stitched centre

Gathered centre

After making the flower, gather the petals made on the inner pegs using a strand of matching thread. Draw up tightly, knot and trim off the ends. Variations can be made by gathering the large petals instead of the small, or by leaving the gathered section a little open making a trumpet shape. In figure 105 the tips of the larger petals have been clipped, sprayed lightly with water, and left to dry.

Over-and-over centre

After stretching the web take the thread through between the petals to the back and up between the opposite petals, back down the first

space and * up in the space next to the opposite one. Repeat from *
working twice round the flower. This results in a ball-like centre
(figure 107).

Fringed edge
Make a basic flower, back stitch and then stem stitch the centre.
Clip the tips off the outer petals and shred them by running a pin
several times through each strand of synthetic raffia from the centre
outwards (figure 103). Alternatively shred the petals made on the
inner pegs instead of the outer pegs (figure 108).

Lacy flower
See diagram 99, figure 106. Attach the thread to the side at space G;
pass it to space H between inner and outer pegs 8; * cross the loom to
space B; then round inner peg 2, outer peg 1 and inner peg 12 to
space L; cross the loom to space E; then round pegs inner 6, outer 7
and inner 8 to space H. Repeat from * until a total of three loops per
petal has been worked.

Move to the next petal position by passing from space H across
the loom to space C; then round pegs inner 3, outer 2 and inner 1 to
space M; cross the loom to space F; then round pegs inner 7, outer 8
and inner 9 to space J. Work the remaining petals similarly.

Work the centre as for the basic flower with both back stitch and
stem stitch. Do not spray with water.

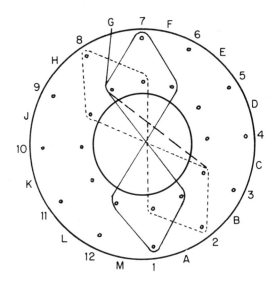

Diagram 99
Stretching the web for a lacy
flower

Figure 105
A flower with a gathered centre
and long petals that have been
clipped and sprayed

Figure 106
A lacy flower with a back stitched
centre

Figure 107
A Catherine wheel flower with an
over-and-over centre

Catherine wheel

See diagram 100, figure 107. Attach the thread to the side at space G; *
cross the loom to space A; then round pegs outer 1 and inner 12 to
space L; cross the loom to space E; then round pegs inner 6 and outer
7 to space G. Repeat from * until there is a total of three loops per
petal.

Move to the next petal position by crossing the loom from space
G to space B; * then round pegs outer 2 and inner 1 to space M; cross
the loom to space F; then round pegs inner 7 and outer 8 to space H;
cross the loom to space B. Repeat from * until there is a total of three
loops per petal. Continue in this way until all the petals have been
worked.

Work the centre in both back stitch and stem stitch. Do not spray
with water.

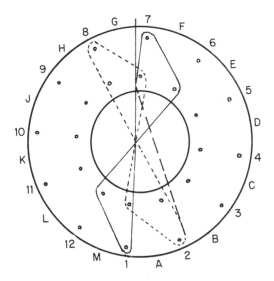

Diagram 100
Stretching the web for a
Catherine wheel

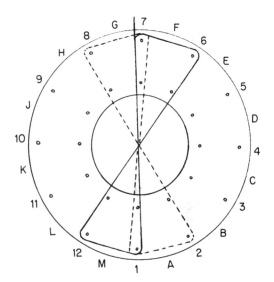

Diagram 101
Stretching the web for a
cartwheel

Cartwheel

See diagram 101, figure 108. Attach the thread to the side at space
G; *cross the loom to space A; then round outer pegs 1 and 12 to
space L; cross the loom to space E; round outer pegs 6 and 7 to space
G. Repeat from * for the required number of loops per petal.

Move to the next petal position by crossing the loom to space B;
*round outer pegs 2 and 1 to space A; cross the loom to space F;
round outer pegs 7 and 8; cross the loom to space B. Repeat from *

for the required number of loops. Continue in this way until all the petals have been worked.

Work the centre in both back stitch and stem stitch. Do not spray with water.

Open cartwheel
See diagram 102, figure 109. An attractive variation consists of only six petals worked as for the Cartwheel. Do not spray with water.

Variations
Vary the appearance of a flower by smoothing out the raffia strands of the large petals (figure 110). Flower loom techniques can also be used to produce imaginative three-dimensional characters and designs, and this can prove an interesting medium for older children to work in (figure 111).

Figure 108
A cartwheel flower with fringed inner petals and a stem stitched centre

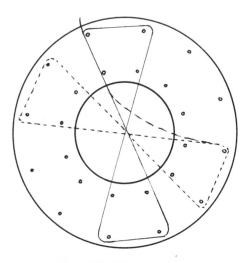

Diagram 102
Stretching the web for an open
cartwheel

Figure 109
An open cartwheel flower with a
stem stitched centre

Figure 110
A flower made as an open
cartwheel with the centre
gathered and the strands of the
outer petals spread open

TEXTURE AND DESIGN

The traditional approach to Teneriffe lace can be modified in many
ways but great care must be taken when designing. The traditional
type of design is comparable to fine etching or the pen and ink
drawings of an artist. Its charm is in the interplay of light and shade.
By using coarser, textured threads and inclusions such as beads, the
character changes and becomes more like the art of the painter in
oils. As the texture and colour of the threads make the work more
busy, so the design needs to become more simple to compensate.
Colour, texture and stitchery must be carefully balanced to form a
harmonious result.

3 Teneriffe lace medallions, edgings and fringe, used to decorate a chair back, cushion and lampshades

4 A white jumper made using a daisy winder, a pink jumper made using a multi-needle, and a pram cover and raffia work made using a flower loom

Figure 111
Synthetic raffia used to make a
fairy decoration, bird and daffodil
using the flower loom

CHAPTER 8

Applications and Mounting

MATS

Lace medallions may be combined to form mats using motifs of the same or different shapes. The medallions may be shaped so that they fit together easily. An oversewing stitch, as explained in chapter 3, is used to join the motifs together. Great care must always be taken when laundering to keep the lace in good condition.

BORDERS

Borders can be made using a series of medallions, usually of the same shape, and linking them together with an oversewing stitch. The border can be attached to material by oversewing through the loops along the edge (see figure 67).

Medallions may also be inset along the edge of the material to make an interesting border, using buttonhole stitch or pin stitch to neaten the edge and attach the lace at the same time. The excess material should be carefully trimmed away with a sharp pair of scissors after the lace has been attached.

Pin stitch

Two small stitches are taken in the same place alternately sewing the edge of the lace to the material and just below the lace. The stitches should be kept small, a large needle should be used and the thread pulled firmly so that the threads of the material are drawn together (diagrams 103–106).

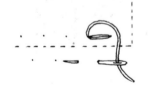

Diagram 103
Working pin stitch—first stage

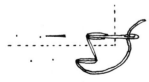

Diagram 104
Working pin stitch—second stage

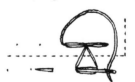

Diagram 105
Working pin stitch—third stage

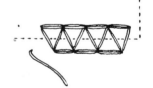

Diagram 106
Working pin stitch—fourth stage

INSERTIONS

Insertions can be made from single or groups of medallions. Buttonhole or pin stitch should be used to attach the lace and to neaten the edge of the material. The excess material is carefully trimmed away after the lace has been attached.

APPLIQUÉ

One or more medallions may be appliquéd onto fabric as required, with the stitches securing the lace to the background by passing the needle through each loop in turn and catching it down. Another method of securing the medallions is by catching down the threads forming the last round of knot stitch. Medallions made in thicker yarns look attractive when appliquéd to cushions (colour plate 3).

MOUNTING

Medallions, fringes and edgings can, of course, be attached to lampshades (figure 80), cushions, window blinds, etc. as trimming, using fabric adhesive. They can also be used to decorate glass jars and other items (figure 112). However, care should be taken when selecting and using the adhesive. It must be used sparingly and preferably only in the centre where the work is thick. Some adhesives turn yellow with age.

Metal brooch and pendant mounts are available from craft suppliers, and are suitable for displaying small medallions. Compact cases, paperweights, glass dishes and ashtrays also provide excellent bases for mounting lace as do silver edged trays. A piece of fine lace made with white thread looks most effective when mounted on black velvet, and this can be framed and covered by glass to make an attractive wall panel.

USING STARCH

To make a mobile, the medallions can be sprayed with starch and allowed to dry before the pins are removed. They will then stay flat and stiff when strung up. Starch is also useful for preparing the medallions for use in collage, on lampshades, or anywhere where a very crisp finish is required. Follow the manufacturer's instructions carefully when applying starch from a spray can or packet.

Figure 112
A glass jar and cork
trimmed with Teneriffe
lace

CHAPTER 9

Alternative Methods of Stretching the Web

SEWN FOUNDATION

The forerunner of Teneriffe lace had its web stretched across a circle of running stitches set in a linen ground. To make the foundation, the plan is drawn on a piece of closely woven material with tailor's chalk (or transferred onto it using dressmaker's carbon paper) and mounted in an embroidery frame. A line of running stitches is worked round the outer circle of the design so that there is one stitch for each ray or spoke of the web. These running stitches are a foundation only and are used to support the web while the embroidery is being worked; they are not part of the finished lace. The foundation thread is usually coloured, so that it shows up when it has to be removed, and strong so that it does not break before the medallion is complete.

The web is stretched by passing the thread from one edge across the wheel of running stitches and outwards under the opposite running stitch, then back under the adjacent stitch, across the wheel, and outwards under the running stitch next to the first one used, and back under the adjacent stitch, and so on until the thread returns to the centre for the last time – one of the spokes of the web being 'missing'. This missing spoke is put in as the embroidery progresses, being the working thread when it passes from one circle of embroidery to the next.

When the embroidery is complete, the medallion is released by cutting the foundation stitches on the wrong side of the material, to avoid damaging the lace. The web may be started from the centre if required.

Variations
Corrugated cardboard can be used instead of linen to form the basis of the wheel (figure 113). Plywood with holes drilled through it also makes a sound base (figure 115).

Double running stitch foundation
An alternative method of making the foundation is to work two lines

125

Figure 113
A wheel made of corrugated
cardboard and a single line of
running stitches

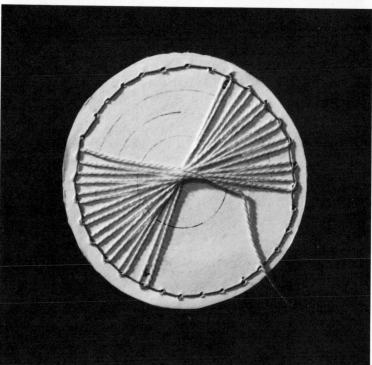

Figure 114
Double running stitch
foundation on corrugated
cardboard

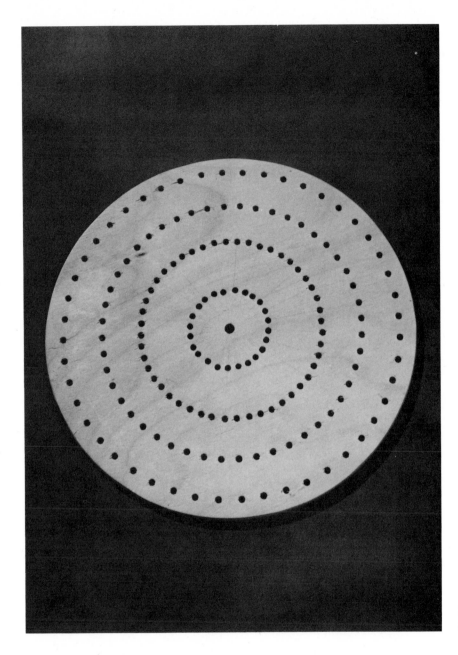

Figure 115
A drilled plywood wheel

of running stitches with the second line filling the spaces between the stitches of the first line (figure 114). The web may be started from the centre of the wheel taking the thread outwards under one running stitch and back under the adjacent stitch; then across the wheel and under the opposite stitch and back under the one adjacent to it, and so on until all the spokes of the medallion are in position.

This method of starting at the centre gives the full quota of 'spokes' in the web, and therefore the working thread must lie alongside one of the 'spokes' when it passes from one round to the next. This method, by which all the spokes are laid at the beginning, is preferable if more than one colour is used.

RIGID WHEELS WITH RADIAL PINS

These wheels consist of two rigid discs, usually metal, with two layers of felt or woollen material sandwiched between them. Pins are inserted between the discs so that they stick out like the rays of the sun. Some discs have marks round the edge to enable the pins to be inserted at regular intervals, and some have concentric circles marked on one side so that the work can be kept even.

A simple version of this wheel can be made at home using two circles of stiff card, two similar circles of batting and a large circle of material, usually velvet, to hold them together. A line of running stitches is worked round the edge of the material which is then placed right side down on the table, and the remaining pieces are arranged in a pile in the centre in the following order: batting, card, batting, card (figure 116).

Figure 116
A rigid wheel with the pins inserted radially

Figure 117
An 'exploded' view of the wheel
in figure 116

The circle of material is drawn over the top layer of card and the
running stitches drawn up tightly and tied off securely (figure 117).
Pins are inserted round the edge into the batting between the two
layers of card.

The web can be stretched to form a complete web, i.e. with all
spokes filled, by starting with a loop reaching from round one pin to
the centre. A slip knot can be used so that the size of the loop is
adjustable. The web is then continued by passing the thread around

the opposite pin, and is completed as usual. An incomplete web, i.e. one with a single spoke missing, can be stretched by starting with the thread tied to one of the pins, then passing it across the wheel and round the opposite pin and so on until all the pins have been used. Of course, the missing spoke will be worked as the embroidery proceeds.

WHEELS WITH TEETH

Many wheels have been made with the edge indented like the teeth of a saw or with small cuts made at regular intervals (figure 118). The materials used for making the wheels include metal, tortoise-shell, plastic, tough rubber and even cardboard. One particular version had metal pegs set around the edge of a rubber disc. Most types have some means of folding the wheel, or bending it to allow the finished medallion to be removed.

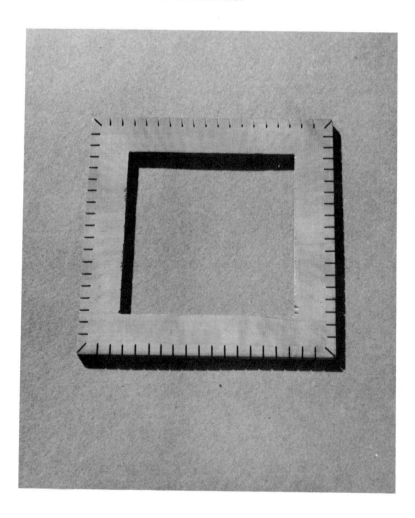

Figure 118
A wooden wheel with 'teeth', shaped to produce a square medallion

RIGID WHEELS WITH VERTICAL PINS

A simple and inexpensive wheel can be made by using corrugated cardboard to make a rigid or semi-rigid base. The design is drawn on paper and pasted onto the cardboard. Pins are pushed vertically through the cardboard at each of the points round the outer circle, and the web stretched across them. The pins can then be pushed so that the heads are flush with the surface of the cardboard (figure 119).

The points of the pins protruding through the wheel should be pushed into a pincushion for safety and strength. A version of this

Figure 119
A corrugated cardboard wheel with vertical pins

was produced commercially consisting of a circle of metal with one or two circles of holes, suitable for pins, punched in it. Each hole was situated in a depression sufficiently large to accommodate the head of the pin. Again a pincushion is necessary with this type of wheel to take the points of the pins.

WOODEN BLOCK WITH NAILS

The design can be drawn onto a piece of wood or paper stuck onto wood, and nails with very small heads hammered part way into the wood to support the web (figure 120).

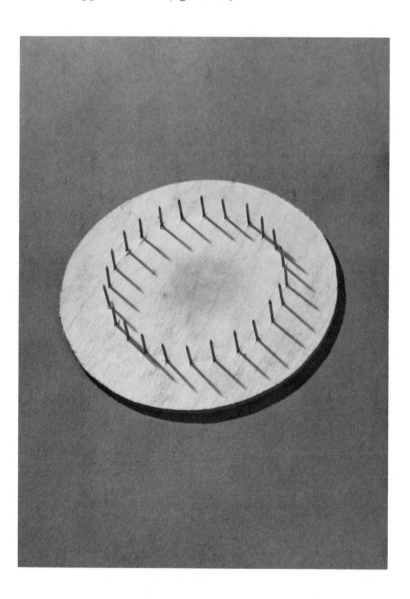

Figure 120
A wooden wheel with vertical nails

Appendix

Diagrams 107 and 108 are polar co-ordinate grids for preparing plans. Diagrams 109 to 115 show various standard plan sizes; the dashes mark opposite points on the plans.

Diagram 107
Polar co-ordinate grid 1

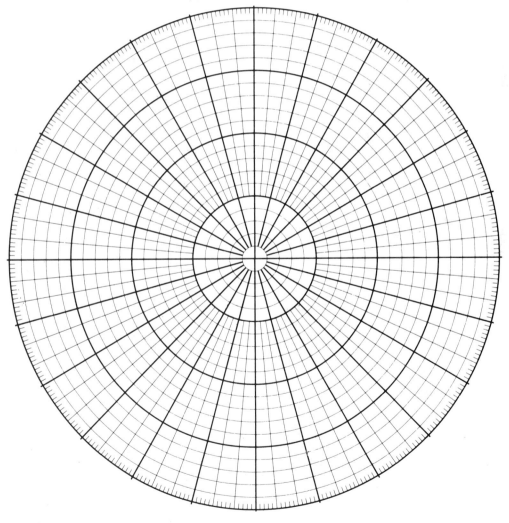

Diagram 108
Polar co-ordinate grid 2

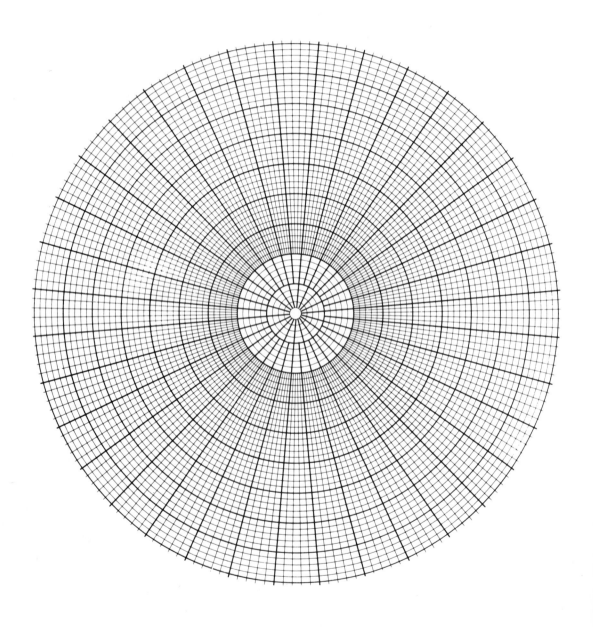

Diagram 109
Wheel plan: 2.5 cm (1 in)
diameter, 24 pins

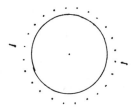

Diagram 111
Wheel plan: 6.25 cm (2½ in)
diameter, 32 pins

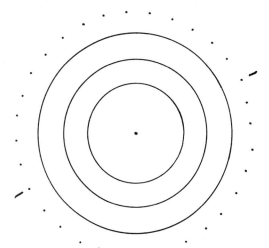

Diagram 110
Wheel plan: 3.2 cm (1¼ in)
diameter, 18 pins

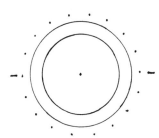

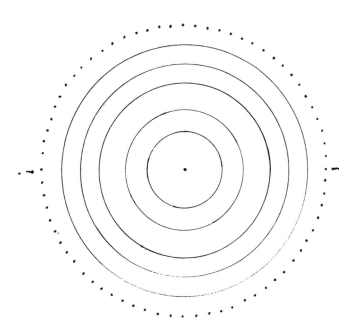

Diagram 112
Wheel plan: 7.5 cm (3 in)
diameter, 72 pins (suitable for use
with star centre diagram 115)

Diagram 113
Wheel plan: 8.75 cm (3⅜ in)
diameter, 48 pins

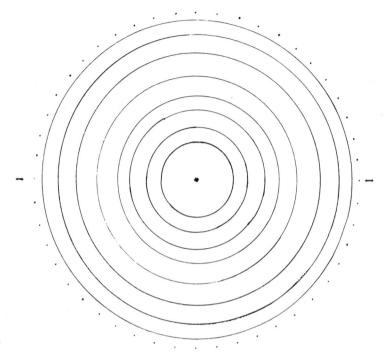

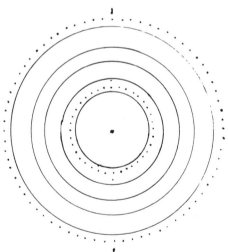

Diagram 114
Wheel plan: Outer ring 6 cm (2⅜
in) diameter, 72 pins; inner ring
2.5 cm (1 in) diameter, 36 pins

Diagram 115
Wheel plan: star centre needing
eight circles to surround it, made
using diagram 112

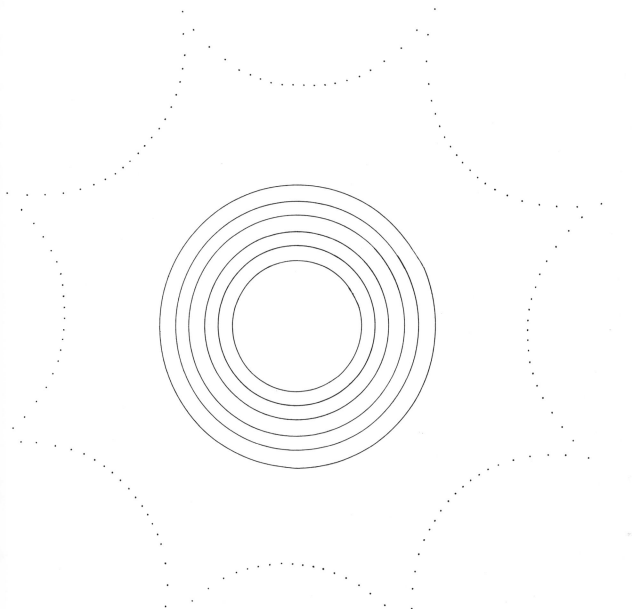

Bibliography

Hispanic Lace and Lacemaking, F. L. May, Hispanic Society of America, 1939

Weldon's Encyclopaedia of Needlework, Waverley, 1942

Teneriffe Lacework, DMC Library, 1923

Encyclopaedia of Needlework, Th. de Dillmont, 1910

Anchor Manual of Needlework, Batsford, 1968

Lace, Virginia Churchill Bath, Studio Vista, 1974

Lacemaking, Eunice Close, Foyles, 1952

Mon Tricot Special—Enjoy Making 1,000 Flowers with a Flower Loom

Swistraw, W. Griffith and Margaret Weymouth, LeJeune, 1974

Suppliers and Addresses

Sources of supply in the UK

A polyurethane foam – markets, DIY shops, craft shops

A needles, thread, pins – needlework shops,

A brooch mounts – craft shops

B paperweights, ashtrays – craft shops and hardware shops

C silver edged trays, jewellery boxes, frames – craft shops, jewellers

D Wendy multi-needle (daisy winder designs can be made on the Wendy multi-needle) – wool shops

E flower loom – wool shops

F polar co-ordinate paper – stationers and office supplies shops

In case of difficulty in obtaining any of the equipment, contact the following suppliers.

ITEMS MARKED A AND C
(postal service)
Mrs A Sells
Lane Cove
49, Pedley Lane
Clifton
Shefford
Beds

ITEMS MARKED B
(postal service)
H Thorn & Sons
118-119 Fore Street
Exeter
Devon
EX4 3JQ

ITEMS MARKED C
(postal service)
Miss D Campbell
Highcliff
Bremilham Road
Malmesbury
Wilts

ITEMS MARKED C (GILT ONLY)
M & M Marketing
83 Hamstead Hall Road
Handsworth Wood
Birmingham B20 1JA

ITEMS MARKED D
(write for nearest stockist)
Carter and Parker Ltd
Guiseley
Yorkshire
LS20 9PD

ITEMS MARKED E
(write for nearest stockist)
H G Twilley Ltd
Roman Mill
Stamford
Lincolnshire PE9 1BG

ITEMS MARKED F
(write for nearest stockist)
H W Peel & Co Ltd
Jeymer Drive
Greenford
Middlesex
UB6 8NX

Sources of supply in the USA
Berga-Ullman Inc
PO Box 918
North Adams
Massachusetts 01247

Frederick J Fawcett
129 South Street
Boston
Massachusetts 02130

Osma Galliger Tod Studio
319 Mendoza Avenue
Coral Gables
Florida 33134

Robin and Russ Handweavers
533 N Adams Street
McMinnville
Oregon 97128

Some Place
2990 Adeline Street
Berkeley
California 94703

The Unique and Art Lace Cleaners
5926 Delmar Boulevard
St Louis
Missouri 63112

Sources of information

Information about lacemaking and classes in the UK can be obtained from the Lace Guild, which may be contacted through the Federation of British Craft Societies at 43 Earlham Street, London WC2H 9LD.

The Lace Society (formerly the Lace Society of Wales) may be contacted through its Chairman, Mrs Amy Straker, 51 Beechley Road, Wrexham, Clwyd.

Information about lacemaking in the USA can be obtained from the International Old Lacers, which may be contacted via Mrs E Reichenbach, 4620–130th SE, Bellevue, Washington 98006. (The English Director is Mrs Joyce R Wilmot, Bramble Mede, 2 Terry Road, High Wycombe, Bucks HP13 6QJ.)

Information about crochet crafts may be obtained from the Crochet Guild, via Miss L Richardson, Pool Foot, Ambleside, Cumbria LA22 9NE.

Please enclose a stamped addressed envelope when sending enquiries to these societies.

Index